The Atoning Death of Christ

FOUNDATIONS FOR FAITH

General editor: Peter Toon

Other titles in the series

The Christian View of Man   H. D. McDonald

FOUNDATIONS FOR FAITH

The Atoning Death of Christ

Ronald S. Wallace

Formerly Professor of Biblical Theology
Columbia Theological Seminary

Crossway Books

To
two generous and loyal friends
John and Jessie Macpherson

Contents

Preface

When Dr Peter Toon approached me a year ago for this contribution to the series *Foundations of the Faith*, he suggested that I should prepare exactly the kind of lecture course I would have given to my own students in my seminary work. I had never ventured to teach on the subject of the Atonement, but I had taken notes, hoping that before I retired I might be able to do so. I was grateful, therefore, for the opportunity of writing for publication the lectures I might have given. The book claims to be no more than the systematic arrangement of the background material necessary to enable a theological student, or a lay person, to take an informed part in the ongoing discussion. But, of course, the lines of thought followed in it are bound to reflect the ways along which my own mind has moved with a measure of understanding and living response as I have tried myself to preach the Gospel and fulfil my own ministry.

The great theologians were never merely academic when they wrote. In order to give some impression of the practical aspects of their response to the cross, in its relevance for our life today, I added to the manuscript some chapters of a more devotional and homiletic nature. These made the book too large for the series, and, indeed, went beyond what I had contracted to do. The publishers, for whose courtesy and helpfulness I am most grateful, have kindly agreed to issue these chapters as a separate and companion book.

I am grateful too, to Dr George Newlands, of the Divinity Faculty of Cambridge University, for his kind concern in putting me in touch with Dr Peter Toon who has also been most helpful. I am again greatly indebted to my daughter, Mrs Heather Finch, not only for typing, but for editing my writing, and making it more clear, condensed, and expressive, than it would otherwise have been. My wife, as ever, has played her own illuminating and encouraging part in the authorship.

Edinburgh
July 1980

Introduction

'What is he for?'

It was Horace Bushnell who provocatively raised the question about Jesus and his death in this form:

> Christ is good, beautiful, wonderful. His disinterested love is a picture in itself; His forgiving patience melts into my feeling. His passion rends open my heart, but what is He for, and how shall he be made to me the salvation I want?

Such questioning had occurred in the early church immediately after he died and it has continued on to this day. Though Jesus' resurrection brought a great measure of release, wonder and joy, the memory of his death plagued the thoughts of the early Christians until the cross itself became what they chiefly gloried in. What, they asked day after day until they had an answer that satisfied them, was the purpose and plan in the mind of God? Why had he brought into the world such a man for the purpose of going through such a death in order to enter his glory?

They discovered the answer gradually from their memories of Jesus' own teaching about himself; from their knowledge and study of the Old Testament scriptures; and through their communion with Jesus during the forty days before his ascension – and the Spirit helped them. It had all to do with our sins, they said: it was God's way of dealing with and destroying the evil of the world in justice and love, in order to bring us to himself.

As they wrote the Gospels these convictions were embodied in the descriptions they handed on of the birth of Jesus, of his life, his miracles and teachings, and especially in their account of how he went to his death and in the details they gave of what happened during his final agonies. The Gospels from beginning to end are oriented to tell us not simply who he was and what he did, but also what he was for. Paul summed up their message: Christ died for our sins according to the Scriptures (1 Cor. 15:3).

The aim of this book is to interpret this text from Paul for ourselves today, first studying as carefully as we can the Old Testament background, and then the most relevant New Testament texts. The fact that we began with a quotation from an American Congregational writer of the nineteenth century (one who in his day was regarded as perhaps dangerously original) is a reminder that we must also put ourselves into debt to whatever of traditional importance has been written about the cross in the history of Christian doctrine.

Faced with all this material from the sources, we will be in a position to suggest guidelines for our thinking on the subject as we face our contemporary situation.

PART 1

THE BIBLICAL DOCTRINE OF ATONEMENT

1 The cross in the Old Testament

SIN, SACRIFICE AND ATONEMENT

The words and phrases used for sin in the Old Testament often liken it to failure to reach the mark, to crookedness in what should be straight, to an uncleanness that people would ordinarily and naturally wish to shun. To sin is to break God's law, whether in those things that demand of us pure, whole-hearted and correct worship, acknowledgement of his truth and goodness, or moral uprightness in our dealings with others.[1]

According to circumstances and in different ages, different kinds of sin were singled out for special condemnation. The great prophets often vigorously condemned it as it appeared in the daily life of the community, in the form of social irresponsibility on the part of the upper classes; of self-aggrandisement on the part of community leaders; of general carelessness for others, especially for the weak and deprived. But at other times the violation of the cultic laws, the neglect or perversion of true worship in the temple were just as forcibly condemned, for all genuine prophets and priests knew that it was what went on in the house of God (or what did not go on there) that determined conduct in the homes, in the council chambers and administration, and in the city streets.

In every age, however insignificant or oppressed an individual might seem to be, he or she was expected to look to God and to live by his law with meticulous care for his honour, and with the deepest concern for any breach in the order of life appointed by him caused by sin. When such a breach occurred it was more serious when the sin was committed 'with a high hand', i.e., presumptuously and deliberately, not only in violation but in defiance of God's known covenant will. But sin often occurred 'unwittingly', i.e. as a careless or even unconscious step into wrong behaviour due chiefly to our human frailty, and

1

cultic laws could be broken almost by accident. Yet even such sin was serious. Its consequences were dreadful, and the offender, whether actively or unwittingly involved, had to seek the restoration and forgiveness provided through the sacrifices and services of the temple. By contrast, sins 'with a high hand' threw the offender outside the sphere in which God is continually gracious.[2]

Sin in its essence was regarded as a violation of the sacred order of life established by God for his people.[3] It was pure self-assertion over against his gracious claim to complete loyalty. His holiness was challenged by it, and his personal bearing and life were insulted by it. He could no longer look upon his people with favour but had to avert his face from the taint of sin and the covert hostility to himself which is often a part of sin, until action was taken to blot out the offence and bring about forgiveness and repentance; to bridge the gulf in personal relations so that people could prove again their loyalty, and a future of renewed trust and friendship could be reopened. Moreover sin seriously threatened God's sovereignty, for it involved an alliance of the sinner with those strange alien forces in the universe that seemed to threaten everything with corruption and annihilation. Inevitably, therefore, when sin occurred in the community, God's will involved a counteracting penalty calculated to destroy all who took pleasure in or reaped profit from what had happened, and indeed all who gave the offending person protection. These nihilistic forces also had to be averted by the community itself, for they too were in danger until the cursed offence was repudiated and fitting amends were made in the destruction of what caused or sheltered offence.

In such critical situations brought between God and man, and thus between man and his environment, it was by means of acts of atonement that the situation was retrieved. By these acts the covenant between God and his people was preserved, God's holiness was re-established, and peace between him and his people was affirmed. It was accepted that atoning acts could also avert the fearful fate that threatened the course of things, redirect the life-forces that determined the future of the individual and community, and cancel the guilt of the past.

Under normal circumstances it was the cultic worship of Israel that gave the community and the individual a regular and established opportunity for putting things right. To the altar in the sanctuary all kinds of sacrifices could be brought and made, and thus sin could be 'covered' or expiated.[4] The evil consequences otherwise brought inevitably by the anger of God could be warded off.

It cannot be overstressed that the sacrifices were regarded as the means provided by God himself in his love for such amends to be made. It was God in his grace who purged iniquity in this way and brought people near to himself in his courts (Ps. 65:3–4). 'God does not demand a cult from which he can reap benefit, but . . . gives his people a cult that enables them to maintain communion with him by means of atonement.'[5] 'The one who atones is God,' says A. B. Davidson.

It may be that in Israel's environment there were many pagan altars where men tried to give utterance to their uneasy consciences and to find in costly sacrifices relief for their own hearts and a means of propitiating the anger of a god. It is possible that sometimes such ideas crept into the minds of men and women in Israel as they, too, sacrificed. But these were ideas to be resisted and prevailed over as Israel came to understand more of God's grace.[6] If they felt as they came to the altar that there was some need to appease the anger of God, they were meant in the actual process of coming and making their sacrifice to find, as the prodigal son himself found, a welcoming love that altered their grudging and small thoughts, and a longing on the part of God that things should be restored to what they were – or made even better. 'In the sacrificial cult' writes von Rad, God 'had ordained an instrument which opened up to her [Israel] a continuous relationship with him. Here Yahweh was within the reach of Israel's gratitude, here Israel was granted fellowship with him in the sacred meal. Above all, here Israel could be reached by his will for forgiveness.'[7]

Of the four types of sacrificial offerings mentioned in the book of Leviticus both the 'peace offering' (3:1–17; 7:11–34), and the 'whole burnt offering' (1:1–17; 6:8–13), along with cereal offerings, were designed to unite the worshippers with God in a shared meal, and to renew or reinforce the relationship between him and his people. The other two types of sacrifice, the 'sin offering' and the 'guilt offering' seem to apply particularly to the more serious breaches of the law, meeting the deepest needs in the minds of the worshippers.[8] The sin offering appears to have been given mainly for offences, possibly involuntary, having to do with matters of ritual. The guilt offering seems to have been given chiefly for offences, often voluntary, having to do with more secular matters such as property.[9] These last two types of sacrifice differed outwardly from each other in the way the blood of the animal was treated. Animal sacrifices could be offered as often as desired by individual supplicants. On special occasions and at the main festivals they were offered on behalf of the whole community.

The major part of the ritual was similar in all the offerings. The animal was brought to the altar, the offerer laid his hands upon the head, the beast was slain, and the blood was treated in a prescribed way, sometimes being smeared on the horns of the altar, sometimes being thrown against the altar, or being poured out at its base. On special occasions it was sprinkled seven times before the mercy seat, and on the mercy seat, and before the veil of the sanctuary. It was a law that the animal should be unblemished.

Undoubtedly, within the life of Israel, those who participated in such sacrifices would have realised that but for the death of such a victim judgment was inevitable. They could not have failed to have it continually impressed on their mind and conscience that, as Eichrodt put it, 'sin is not forgiven as a matter of course, but as the result of the offering of a pure and innocent life as expiation for the guilt-laden life of the offerer.'[10]

When we seek to understand the meaning of these rites we enter the realm of conjecture. The Old Testament itself gives us no explanation why the offerer should lay his hand on the head of his animal. Some scholars see in this rite simply the dedication of the offering. Those who believe that the details of the Old Testament rites must contain foreshadowings of the way in which Christ himself in his sacrifice bore our sins, see the rite as full of deeper significance: by laying his hand on the head of the animal with confession of sin the worshipper is identifying himself with the victim in an action that symbolises the transfer of sin to the offering. 'What happens to the animal happens symbolically to himself . . . the death is his own death, accepted by him as the consequence of his sin.' More cautiously, von Rad says, 'We would give very much to know the significance of the laying of hands on the head.'[11]

The only explanation given in the Old Testament of the significance of the blood and its use is in the text of Leviticus: 'For the life of the flesh is in the blood; and I have given it for you upon the altar to make atonement for your souls: for it is the blood that makes atonement by reason of the life' (17:11). In the same passage it is emphasised that God has banned every other use of blood by his people: it is reserved exclusively for his own purposes, so that he can make it such a prominent, possibly symbolic, element in the means he has ordained for the expiation of sins. When the Israelite makes his offering and sees the blood his thoughts are directed to the life that is now being poured out in death for his sake.

It is noticeable that even those scholars who might be expected to find the closest links between the thought of the Old Testament and the New find little justification in the text of the Old Testament for asserting that the sacrificed animal was regarded as vicariously bearing the punishment of the guilty offerer and as thus in some sense satisfying God's justice.[12] Such vicarious bearing of guilt is certainly suggested in part of the ritual of the Day of Atonement (Lev. 16). On this great annual national occasion two goats were presented to the priest and were then set apart by means of drawn lots for quite opposite fates. One was destined to be sacrificed at the altar for the Lord. On the head of the other, the priest laid his hand and confessed the sins of the people. The animal was then driven out to carry all the iniquities of the nation upon itself into the waste land. Yet scholars note that even if there is encouragement to interpret this ceremony as the transference of guilt and penalty from the people to the scapegoat, nevertheless the guilt in this instance is not transferred to the goat actually sacrificed.[13] Most Old Testament scholars at this point do not attempt to give explanations. 'The sacramental act expiates,' says Vriezen, 'because God wants to use it as such.'[14]

We have seen that the sacrificial ritual of the temple was designed to deal only with sins committed without deliberate intention.[15] But those who felt that their sins put them beyond the help offered in the temple could still find comfort in the fact that God could provide atonement for both misdemeanours and more serious sins outside the cultic life of the community. If forgiveness was indeed based on God's good pleasure and signified his grace, then there was hope that such grace would not be limited in its possibilities or confined to the religious spheres of life. Thus we find written within a catalogue of purely judicial matters that a man can 'redeem his life' even in a case of a fault deserving of death, by paying a money ransom (Exod. 21:30). And on certain occasions the local rulers were provided with means of expiating the guilt of their community when it was suspected that it was harbouring serious crime. Such a ritual of atonement involved breaking the neck of a heifer in a valley with running water. It was a ritual quite different from any in the temple, but it too was God's way of 'removing the guilt of innocent blood' in their midst (Deut. 21:1–9).

When we turn to the historical narratives, especially of the early life of Israel with God, we find other examples of sin being atoned for by rites quite different from those of the religious cult. When Israel made and worshipped the golden calf, and when, later, they 'yoked themselves with Baal of Peor' and 'played the harlot with the daughters of Moab', these were undoubtedly occasions of 'high-handed' rebellion against the covenant by a significant majority of the community (Num. 25:1–13). God's anger was roused and some fearful punishment was immediately given, but not such as by God's previous warning the seriousness of the sin deserved. In both places the plague was stayed and the sin was expiated. How this happened is instructive.

In the case of the golden calf, Moses was encouraged to pray at the same time as God forbade him to pray: 'Let me alone, that my wrath may burn hot' (Exod. 32:10). Moses is pleading with God to cool things down. God gently asks him to desist and at the same time assures him that his prayer is being only too effective! So Moses continued on and on passionately interceding for mercy, and as he pleaded he felt the burden of the nation's guilt so deeply that he offered his own exclusion from the book of life as a substitute for the dreadful fate that threatened Israel (Exod. 32:31–2). God then accepted Moses' inspired intercession as expiation. In the case of the idolatry at Baal of Peor, Phinehas was inspired by the jealousy of God himself to a bloody and symbolic act of ritual which 'made atonement for the people' (Num. 25:10–12).

During the reign of David two other noticable examples of the covering of sin took place. At a time of famine David was called on to make expiation because he heard from God that the blood-guilt of Saul's treachery against the Gibeonites was still adversely affecting the life of the kingdom (2 Sam. 21:3ff. When the Gibeonites were asked, they called for the death of seven sons of Saul, who were slain and the famine was stayed. And at another later time of plague David himself made intercession, for it was his fault that had brought on the trouble (2 Sam. 24:1ff). He offered, as Moses had done, to take the whole punishment upon himself and his father's house. The prayer coincided with God's repenting of the evil and staying the hand of 'the angel who was working destruction' (vv. 16–17).

In all these extra-ritual acts of expiation the underlying ideas emerge more clearly than in the case of the temple ritual: the passion and death and zeal of one can be substituted for the passion or death or zeal of another, and a ransom can be paid for deliverance from guilt. This pattern of thought, so basic in Israel, found expression in the words of a later prophet:

For I am the Lord your God,
  the Holy One of Israel, your Savior.
I give Egypt as your ransom,
  Ethiopia and Seba in exchange for you.
Because you are precious in my eyes,
  and honoured, and I love you,
I give men in return for you,
  peoples in exchange for your life (Isa. 43:3–4).

And note from this citation that it is God himself who provides the ransom.

The important point made at some stage in most of the narratives and emphasised in the extra-ritual atoning acts, is that God shares and inspires the concern that the sin and its consequences should be wiped out. If the consideration that God's anger has to be propitiated is present, it is there as a fugitive thought. Yet God's judgment on sin is always there in these acts of atonement, even alongside his forgiving love, and sometimes as the background for the exercise of his forgiving love. Karl Barth points out that in Isaiah 6, 'it is not after but in the manifestation of judgment that there comes the pardon, reconciliation, calling and conversion of the prophet.'[16]

In all the atoning acts of forgiveness God's 'wrath' is expressed in the measure of suffering that accompanies the act, but its expression is only partial and it is restrained at the crucial moment. Throughout the whole of the Old Testament this is shown to be a habit with God. His wrath is 'but for a moment' and compared with the eternity of his love. He does not execute its fierceness.[17]

> Yet he, being compassionate,
> forgave their iniquity,
> and did not destroy them;
> he restrained his anger often,
> and did not stir up all his wrath.
> He remembered that they were but flesh . . . (Ps. 78:38–9)

The force of such passages in the Old Testament made A. B. Davidson affirm that in divine wrath there is 'not an attribute like righteousness, but rather a transient affection'.[18] Another great Old Testament scholar in a comment on Psalm 30:5 writes: 'Since it is the wrath of God, we should take it very seriously. But just because it is the wrath of *God*, it springs from a reality which is different from that from which the anger of man springs. It is not something that is ultimate and final. The purpose of God's anger is not to destroy but to educate.'[19]

The educative exercise of God's wrath can be illustrated by the case of David's own sin with Bathsheba. The sin of David was 'put away' by a simple prophetic word (so free and gracious is the forgiving love of the Lord!). Yet in being forgiven David entered a long path of suffering in which, partly because of his continuing folly, and partly because we human beings should always become aware of something of the cost of our sin and forgiveness, like a greater one to come, he

7

'learned obedience' (Heb. 5:8. Cf. 2 Sam. 12:1–15; 16:20–2; 18:33). In David's case the chastening and suffering was laid on him after the word of forgiveness came to him. To the generation addressed in Isaiah 40 the word of forgiveness came after years of bitter exile at the end of a period of suffering that in the grace of God was called 'double measure' for all their sins (Isa. 40:2, NEB).

Of course it must be added that what matters most to God in all the offerings and acts of atonement is the sincere expression of repentance and concern on the part of the offerer or the mediator, and this involves the humble and contrite acceptance of whatever measure of due suffering God wills to allow to come upon the guilty. That is why intercession, even of the mediator, is always accompanied by a deep undertone of personal confession. If all this is lacking and the outward ritual becomes merely perfunctory, then the whole system of sacrifice can be so useless as to be called an abomination to the Lord (Isa. 1:11–15).

FORMS OF MEDIATION

Occasional acts of atonement were brought about by 'lay' people like Phinehas, but most often the task of expiation was undertaken by priests, prophets or kings whose chief rôle in the community was to act as mediator. This was a unique rôle and it has several aspects relevant to our understanding of the New Testament.

The priest

The priest's main duty was to act as a go-between for both God and man. Especially he acted as an agent in the offering of the sacrifices which restored the personal relationship between God and the individual and re-established the threatened covenant between God and his people. Priests received the gifts, made the offerings, manipulated the blood, and led the people in their required ritual. To adapt a New Testament phrase: they were mediators of the old covenant (Heb. 9:15).

The priests were expected to be teachers. They ensured that the correct ritual was observed, and interpreted to the people what God was saying to them in the sacramental worship and the tradition behind the feasts. They were to teach that the sacrifices were simply signs of true repentance and new obedience. Therefore we occasionally see them reading the law to the people, interpreting it, and giving instruction in its duties (Deut. 31:9ff; 2 Chron. 17:7–9; Ezek. 22:26; 44:23). When they failed in their tasks as teachers God raised up the prophets to take over this aspect of their work.

As well as being teachers the priests were expected to live an exemplary life in the community, scrupulously observing the law they had to teach. They were expected to have a separation and holiness which reflected that of God himself into whose near presence they so often came. When they failed they were allowed to sink to the worst possible depths of depravity and came under relentless judgments (1 Sam. 1–4).

The office of priest came to belong peculiarly to the tribe of Levi. They were regarded as the group elected by God for this purpose, and special economic provisions were made by statute so that they could become the holy, separate brotherhood that was required. It has been hailed as one of the miracles and mysteries of the Old Testament that a tribe whose forefather acted with disgraceful treachery in the affair of Dinah and Shechem, and earned his father's curse upon his anger (Gen. 34), should later be able to rehabilitate itself and prove its worth in an outstanding act of atoning zeal in the affair of the golden calf, and presumably in other incidents at Meribah and Massah (Exod. 32:26ff; Deut. 33:8–10). The tribe of Levi came to be recognised by God himself as prepared to disown their brothers in order to keep the covenant. Their atoning zeal in times of crisis made it fitting that they should be chosen to minister God's expiating love within the temple.

In offering the sacrifices the priests were regarded as both representing Israel, standing before God on behalf of his people (Deut. 10:8), and making the offering while the rest remained in passive acknowledgement of what was being done in their name. In some such way as the firstborn of a family was claimed by God as a representative for the whole family, so the Levites were regarded by God as representing the nation (Exod. 13:2; 22:29; 30:20; Num. 3:12–13; 8:6–14). S. H. Hooke has called the Levites 'a corporate substitute for sinful and rebellious Israel'.[20] They were to regard themselves as in solidarity not only with their congregation but also with the victims which were offered on the altar in sacrifice, for it was an important part of the ritual that they ate the flesh of the sacrifice.[21] In their representative capacity before God the priests' duty was to make intercession for those whose sacrifice they offered. It was a duty, like that of teaching, grossly neglected (Joel 2:17; Mal. 2:7–8). This task also the prophets had to take over from them.

The prophet

The prophets seem to have acted as the continuing conscience of Israel, taking up the tasks in which the priests had failed. They recalled the nation to the true meaning of the covenant, the law, the sacrifices, and the temple itself. They lived in the counsel of God, interpreting history by his inspiration, delivering for their times his word in his name (Num. 24:3ff; Jer. 23:18, 22; Amos 3:7–8). They preached with his authority and, indeed, were to be regarded as speaking with his voice (Hos. 12:10; Isa. 55:11). They had to stand, as the priests often failed to do, on God's side, representing him and his truth over against the rebellious people of the day, and bearing the antagonism that was directed at him. They suffered acutely when the word they preached clashed, as it often did, with the mainstream of current hopes, policy and opinion in the nation. They often found themselves alone, ostracised and completely misunderstood. They were even conspired against and persecuted. All this, as von Rad says, 'made deep inroads into their personal lives and even imperilled their whole existence'.[22]

Some of the harsh implications of the prophetic ministry of suffering on the side of God can be illustrated from Ezekiel's own account. His task was to warn his people of the future misery they might incur if they went on disobeying God; of coming siege, captivity and famine. Today we can be brought face to face with the stark horror of what famine and siege and war can bring by pictures in our news media. Ezekiel was to enact the meaning of his word in his own life. He was to experience the reality of the doom he was proclaiming so intensely that as he preached he was to eat his bread with quaking and drink water with trembling and fearfulness. As he warned of siege and captivity he had to lie on his left side for a hundred and ninety days to 'bear the sin' of north Israel, and then on his right side for a further forty days to bear the sin of Judah (Ezek. 4:4–8). When warning of coming famine he had to starve himself for a period corresponding to the length of the threatening ordeal, feeding only on famine rations weighed out carefully before onlookers and cooked on dung. Such 'unclean bread' would be the kind eaten in a foreign land by people starved and in captivity (vv. 9–17). On another occasion he was urged by God to work himself up to a frenzy. He was to 'cry' and 'howl', beating his breast with remorse because the word he was to deliver to others was so piercing it had to become to himself a sharp sword lacerating his heart (21:12). These are tasks he has to force himself to. If not God will compel him in other ways (4:7–8).

We must try to gain insight into what all this was supposed to mean.

There was the physical strain of living at a high emotional pitch, without being allowed to relax. We can imagine the sheer weariness, boredom, and abject humiliation involved in the sign of lying on his side in public for months on end; and disgust and nausea caused by living in an unclean way on meagre food. We see this strange, mad fellow, a local spectacle, gaunt, emaciated and pathetic, and we are reminded of the pictures of starving people from war and famine areas today.

The actions which Ezekiel was told to perform as he preached the word were called signs: indeed the prophet himself was a sign. The signs were symbols of the coming judgment he was to preach about. Through them the prophet was to feel 'his solidarity with human misery'.[23] What makes these actions so significant for us in a study that moves, of course, towards the New Testament, is the word that accompanied the instruction to Ezekiel to lie on his side: 'I will lay the punishment of the house of Israel upon you' (Ezek. 4:4). This can be interpreted: 'The coming disaster is casting its shadow before, and harnessing the prophet, body and soul alike, with a hard yoke of suffering.'[24]

Suffering came to many of the prophets not by prescription but by persecution (cf. Jer. 20; Amos 7:10ff). But it was in inner feeling that some of them suffered most. Ezekiel is reserved on this matter, and it is in Jeremiah's book that we see the inward cost of serving the word of God. Jeremiah seems to have shared something of the suffering of God himself in having to inflict punishment. He was sensitive to the mockery and reproach that were brought upon him when he delivered his message. But more clearly than ever before another strange aspect of prophetic suffering is apparent: in his solidarity with his people the prophet also had to share in his heart the suffering of even the 'wicked' on whom he had to pronounce judgment.

We see a sympathetic agony seizing Moses when he protested to God that he was going too far in judgment; we see it in Elijah too (Exod. 32:11–20; 1 Kings 17:20). But in Jeremiah, more sensitive and self-revealing than any of his predecessors, the burden seems to be greatly intensified, and it lies behind many of the complaints and protests to God that are scattered through his book (cf. chapters 11–20). Jeremiah's sense of oneness with the people at times was so acute that, as von Rad says, 'the clash between Yahweh and his disobedient people took place within the prophet himself.'[25] Instead, then, of seeing him stand over against the people on the side of God, we see him standing on the side of humanity over against God.

In their mediatorial capacity the prophets are both on the side of

God and on the side of the people. It is this fact that makes them above all the great intercessors of the Old Testament. It was accepted that it was the prophet's duty to pray for the nation.[26] No doubt it is in reference to this that Ezekiel describes the true prophet as one who could 'stand before' God 'in the breach', and thus 'defend the land from ruin' (22:28ff; cf. 13:4–5).

Intercession in the suffering prophet is linked up with 'bearing the sin' of the people (Isa. 53:12). 'There is a solidarity between those men and the people,' writes A. B. Davidson. 'Their confession of the people's sin is the people's confession. And yet they are different. They are near to God. He has respect to them. Their intercession usually sets before God those great motives in himself from which he acts – his confession, his covenant, his redemptive work already begun, his name's sake, his sole Godhead, yet his being "known alone to Israel".'[27]

The king

God eventually allowed Israel to have kings as well as priests and prophets. They, too, represented the people before God, approaching him on their behalf and praying for them (2 Sam. 24:17; 1 Kings 8:22ff; 2 Chron. 14:11; Isa. 37:14ff). God also made a covenant with the king on behalf of the nation, and sought through the king to bestow blessing as well as protection, justice and welfare on the whole nation (2 Sam. 7:5–17; 23:5; Ps. 72:1–12).

The king represented God to the people. God himself was called king. The majesty and glory surrounding the earthly king were pointers to the majesty and glory of God himself in his heavenly court (1 Kings 22:19; Ps. 84:3; Isa. 6:5).

THE EMERGING PATTERN FOR THE FUTURE

The people of Israel in early times, particularly just after they had settled in the promised land, tended to look backwards. When Joshua, for instance, renewed the covenant with them at Shechem, and appealed to them to rededicate themselves to God, he recited the great things God had done for them in their past – in the times of the patriarchs and during the exodus and the wilderness wanderings (Josh. 24:7 ff). Samuel, too, years later, cast their minds back in a similar evocation (1 Sam. 12:7 ff). It was common practice in their prayers to challenge God to be as gracious to them as he had been to their forefathers at the Red Sea or at Sinai or in the deserts. Elijah on his great day at Carmel knew no better mould in which to cast himself than that of Moses recalling Israel to the God of Abraham, Isaac and Jacob, and seeking the same fire from heaven as had encouraged his great predecessor (1 Kings 18:21 ff).

But in the reign of King David when Israel's national prosperity was at its peak, an even more glorious era was prophesied. This was to be presided over by a successor of David – an offspring of his house – on a throne established eternally before God in a kingdom of peace and unparalleled prosperity (2 Sam. 7).

Many began to wonder what this new world might mean for their future, and slowly the focus and orientation of thought in the nation began to change. Such a clear promise of future greatness made them look forward, and indeed, they even began to think that this wonderful messianic era might be just round the corner. With each birth of a new heir to the throne they asked, could this be the birth of the great anointed one? But king succeeded king, and they seemed on the whole to grow worse. Some were weak in their faith, others bungled things or were simply unfortunate, and all hope for progress to a future era seemed to be dashed.

In such circumstances we might expect to find increasing pessimism and cynicism, and harking back to past glories. Instead something quite extraordinary happened to the prophets of Israel.[28] Things, they said, would not go on and on in a continual process of corruption. God would step in with a mighty act of well planned disaster. There would be a tribulation inconceivable and terrible, involving all nations. God would use the worst nations as instruments for cleansing his people, and then destroy the instruments he had exalted. In the midst of this cataclysm of judgment God would begin to fulfil all the promises he had given to the house of David on a scale more glorious than ever dreamed of before. The great events of their past history, they now said, held as much hidden meaning for the future as the former glory of the house of David and his city Jerusalem. In this new messianic age there was ordained for the people of God not only a new David, a new Jerusalem, and a new temple, but also a new exodus, a new entry into a new promised land under a new covenant – indeed, for God's people there would be a new creation: mankind would be given a new heart.

Faced with social collapse in Israel the later great prophets found it increasingly difficult to apply the ideals and standards of the past to the present. They saw before them the human situation and the human heart incurably ailing. They gave up all hope of restoring the past, and ceased to look for any transforming development in things as they were. But they became more and more certain that all the promises of God to their nation were going to be fulfilled in a new unknown way through creative acts of God never before dreamed of as possible. Sometimes they felt in their own hearts, and saw signs around them, that the new had already begun:

> Remember not the former things,
>   nor consider the things of old.
> Behold, I am doing a new thing;
>   now it springs forth, do you not perceive it? (Isa. 43:18–19)

They continued to take inspiration and encouragement from the past in their great new expectation, for the new era was to come about under the same power as had accomplished the old. Moreover, in 'former things' they found the patterns God was going to follow in the new future. Indeed, their whole past history under God was to be repeated, but transformed. The earlier events were themselves prophecies or 'types' of the greater events to come.

This prophetic linking of the past to the future has led to what is often called the 'typological' interpretation of the Old Testament, the basic principle being that God in the past showed the shape of future events not simply through oracles but through the pattern of his working in the nation's history; in the lives of chosen individuals within the nation; and in the institutions and customs at the centre of its religious life. As E. Earle Ellis puts it: God 'moulds and uses history' in order to 'reveal and illumine his purpose. God writes his parables in the sands of time.'[29]

The finding of prototypes in the earlier history of Israel which foreshadow and correspond to things to come, was taken up by the New Testament writers who saw the Old Testament 'full of pointers and predictions of the Christ event'. Their approach to the Old Testament was 'based on the assumption that all Israel's experience of Yahweh had been planned with reference to Jesus Christ,'[30] and, of course, when they gave him the title 'the Messiah', 'the Christ' ('the Anointed One'), they were acknowledging that he was the glorious redeemer to whose future coming the prophets' hopes had been lifted so strangely and wonderfully, as all their false hopes vanished.

As we have indicated, this typological exegesis did not confine itself to the pattern set by the monarchy, or by the great historical acts of the exodus and the wilderness wanderings. It did not hesitate to find the pattern which Jesus fulfilled also in the figures of the great prophets, especially in their sufferings and intercessions, and it extended to finding deeply etched parallels between the action and intention of the temple priests offering their sacrifices in former times, and that of Jesus going to his cross. Moreover they found all the Old Testament acts of atonement meaningful in understanding his sacrifice.

At this point it has to be noted that the same prophetic circle which gave glorious pictures of the new exodus, the new covenant, the new age of glory, and the new king, also gave an unforgettable picture of a suffering servant of God, partly prophet, partly priest. It occurs in a series of four oracles in the later chapters of the book of Isaiah, culminating in chapter 53 (42:1–14; 49:1–6; 50:4–9; 52:13–53:12). In the first oracle he is pointed out to us by God and described. In the second and third he is present with us, speaking to us intimately, revealing his mind as if he were a friend. In the final oracle he has died, and the meaning of his life and death – especially of the unique death he suffered – is being described to us by some of those who misunderstood and persecuted him, but who have since found God, forgiveness, and new life through what he suffered.

We hear him say to us that he knows himself called and drawn close to God from his mother's womb. He is kept hidden by God like a favourite arrow in the quiver of a warrior reserved for use in winning a great prize and a decisive conflict (49:1–2). In the sight of God, whom he never fails to please, he is to have glory and to win more glory (49:3; 52:13). He is to establish justice on earth, to be a 'light to all nations and salvation to the ends of the earth' (42:4; 49:6). He accepts the task. God's word of assurance is his only comfort and reward on this earth (49:4; 50:7–9); for with men he is destined to win only shame, misunderstanding, hatred, treachery and condemnation to such mutilation in his death that even the hardened and cruel are startled and ashamed (52:14—53:3). Yet he gives his cheek to the smiters and makes his complaint only to God, praying for his persecutors. To fight his enemies, to win followers and further the cause of God he has to use only the quiet and gentle weapons of speech and suffering (42:2). God opens his ear daily and gives him his words for the weary and the weak (50:4). It is they who find that he alone understands and helps them, and they alone recognise his worth and take his help (42:3). We learn that after his death, those who told of his death, and others who heard, came to understand that somehow in his death he was bearing the sin not only of those who struck him, but of 'many' (53:12).

But he was wounded for our transgressions,
    he was bruised for our iniquities;
upon him was the chastisement that made us whole,
    and with his stripes we are healed.
All we like sheep have gone astray;
    we have turned every one to his own way;
and the Lord has laid on him
    the iniquity of us all (53:5–6).

Who was he and how did we come to have this haunting description of him? Many features of his career and ministry are like those of other great prophets, and S. H. Hooke believes that the prophet of the exile responsible for Isaiah 40–55, 'Deutero-Isaiah', is described by his disciples in these poems which they inserted within the collection of his oracles. He makes the comment: 'It was no new thing that a prophet's death should have been interpreted by a contemporary in the way it is here.'[31] Von Rad finds the nearest Old Testament parallel to this man in Moses as depicted in the book of Deuteronomy (he believes that Moses was described there as fulfilling a ministry of 'complete vicarious mediation'), and he adds 'both [Deuteronomy and the servant passages] outline the picture of a mediator that was never realised in the span of the Old Testament saving history.'[32]

Whether the Old Testament picture was one of an ideal only to be realised in the messianic age, or the dedicated account by some disciple of his own master, we have to agree that here 'in secret a mould was being prepared into which the experience of Jesus was to be poured.'[33]

The prophets carried into their vision of the future yet other features of the pattern from the past which are relevant to our study of atonement. One of these is the feature of the 'remnant'. The whole community of the people of God would have to be tested and sifted before the new age could come (Amos 9:8–10). The standards God expected of daily conduct before him, and of loyalty under stress, would prove too high for most of those who glibly professed to belong to him. Those who passed them would be only a 'remnant'. Early in the history of the nation only Joshua and Caleb survived out of their generation to lead the people into the promised land. And in Elijah's day only seven thousand out of all Israel were numbered by God as his own (Num. 14:26–31; 1 Kings 19:18).

It was Isaiah who most clearly saw the election of a surviving, faithful remnant as a chief feature of Israel's entry into the new age. The idea was lodged in his mind from the day of his call, and he felt it was divinely given. He named one of his children 'a remnant shall return' because he wanted to impress his conviction on his contemporaries: 'Though your people Israel be as the sand of the sea, only a remnant of them will return' (6:11–13; 7:3; 10:22). He described the survival of this remnant dramatically and vividly in his poems. And he gathered and nurtured a little community of the faithful around himself and his teaching, as if even this were the beginning of the work of God in gathering it together (8:5–18).

Later prophets kept the tradition before them during the crisis that led to the exile (Zeph. 2:3–9; 3:13). Yet though there were high hopes that those who returned from Babylon after the captivity might show the characteristics of the elect, such hopes were dashed. The fulfilment of the pictures of the true people of God coming out from among the nations who had overwhelmed them, and forming together a new and close community (Ezek. 36:24 ff; Mal. 3:16) had to wait for fulfilment in the 'latter days', along with the other great visions of the future.

It may be that another picture of this 'remnant' deliberately thrown into the ultimate future, is given to us in 'the saints of the most high' who, at the end of all the conflicts among the nations, are seen as sharing in the triumph and kingdom of the 'Son of man' who is at that juncture himself to come 'with the clouds of heaven' to receive everlasting dominion (Dan. 7:27, 13).

2 The cross in the mind and purpose of Jesus

THE KINGDOM OF GOD IS AT HAND!

We have no account of how, where and when John the Baptist heard his call to become the prophet and forerunner of the Messiah. Some imagine that he belonged to a desert sect similar to the Essenes, or to the sect which produced the Qumran documents, and that his ministry was inspired by membership of such a community. Some think that he often went by himself into the wilderness to brood and to pray, and received his commission there in the same way as Elijah his predecessor received his. But is it not possible that what influenced John the Baptist most was his early training and worship in the synagogue? It was the custom to read the great prophecies about the future along with the law and the other writings. Their message was taught to the people, and they were considered an important part of traditional liturgy, treasured as historical, poetical and theological documents. In them the Jews of the first century found their roots, their best literature, their formative ideas about God. And the faithful heard about a future which they hoped would one day come to pass.

John must have been there often, listening. He had reason to be specially interested: somehow he realised that the days he was living through might be the 'last days'. His godly mother must have shared this current view with him as she also shared with him the strange experiences and intimations that had come to her just before he was born. Perhaps he was still a youngster when the inescapable and constraining conviction of his ministry began to form in his mind. We can picture him, indeed, intent as Donatello imagined him in his unforgettable bronze statue in Florence. At any rate, he listened to the readings in the synagogue differently from anyone else. It was as if God himself was again speaking directly to him the very words he had originally spoken to the great prophets. Their oracles came to him in such a way that they could no longer be considered liturgy, but had to be heard as announcement. The words in his mind were no longer simply pieces of poetry to 'teach and delight and move' the mind and heart, but were a clear, detailed programme of what God was soon going to bring about around him. Indeed, they became for him the kind of thing we find in our newspapers as a catalogue of 'forthcoming events'.

It was his burning conviction of the imminence of the events described in the oracles that constituted his call to be himself one of the prophets. Jesus justly described him not only as the last but as the greatest of them. For, after all, each of John's predecessors had passed on to posterity only a few aspects of the whole message about what was to come. John's task was greater – to announce the completed message. Each of these prophets had died before his pronouncements could be tested. John was to stand up and tell the surrounding world to look about them in order to see it all happening here and now. And when the time for the announcement came he was to proclaim himself the one appointed by God as initiator. He had simply to wait for the signal.

His message was to be 'The kingdom of God is at hand!' The promises of all the prophets about the new coming age were soon to be fulfilled in a literal way. It was news the weak, the oppressed and the humble in every age had been waiting for – the day of their vindication and liberation! No more war; instead, universal peace and justice according to the law of Israel's God. No more corruption and decay, for death too was to be destroyed. Paradise was to be restored in the place of conflict, cruelty and desert places. The Messiah was to come, and men and women were to see 'the king in his beauty' – the one who would establish justice everywhere, eternally.

There was, of course, the other side of the message. Only for those who feared and believed would the 'sun of righteousness arise with healing in his wings'. For others the day was to be one of darkness: 'For behold, the day comes, burning like an oven, when all the arrogant and all evildoers will be stubble; the day that comes shall burn them up, says the Lord of hosts, so that it will leave them neither root nor branch' (Mal. 4:1–3).

While waiting for the word of God to come to him we can imagine John preparing his strategy in his mind. Some details of his task were clear to him from the Scriptures. He was to model his preaching and action on Elijah's, for Malachi had clearly taught that before the 'great and terrible day of the Lord', God would send back 'Elijah the prophet' (4:5). Indeed, there was a current belief that Elijah was to return in person before the Messiah came.

John saw that his first task was to gather together the 'remnant' from among the people – those who were ready to turn to the Lord (Isa. 10:20–3). He would call on them from among the cities and villages to 'flee from the wrath to come', and by their repentance to make themselves ready to enter the new age, and be re-adopted as the people of God.

The wilderness of Judea was to be the scene of his ministry. The remnant, he felt, should be gathered together in a place quite apart from their city or village life – for what would remain of that life when the winnowing fire came, and the axe fell on all the political and ecclesiastical establishments? Moreover, the prophetic oracles of the new age had often depicted its effect on the wilderness – trees and fruit would grow; rivers and fountains would appear; and the Messiah, when he came, would preside over a great banquet for his people, repeating the miracle of the manna in the wilderness. John heard himself summoned to be a 'voice . . . crying in the wilderness: Prepare the way of the Lord, make his paths straight.' So in the traditions of Elijah, the wilderness prophet, he went there, wearing 'a garment of camel's hair, and a leather girdle around his waist; and his food was locusts and wild honey' (Matt. 3:1–5).

He completed his plans with a decision which has left its permanent mark on the Christian church, and in which we have to see direct divine inspiration. Since he had been called to form around him the nucleus of a true, purified community, he would call on its members to accept an outward sign – or sacrament – that they believed the message and accepted its implications. John probably took his inspiration and authority to devise this sign of baptism from the prophecy of Ezekiel about the remnant:

> For I will take you from the nations, and gather you from all the countries, and bring you into your own land. I will sprinkle clean water upon you, and you shall be clean from all your uncleannesses, and from your idols I will cleanse you. A new heart I will give you, and a new spirit I will put within you; and I will take out of your flesh the heart of stone and give you a heart of flesh (Ezek. 36:24–6).

If people were prepared to meet the demands of his preaching to revolutionise their thought and life, and repent, it was important that there be a public sign of their resolution. It would be, at least, a sign that God according to his word was going to give them the new heart and spirit.

We wish we had more exact information about how John in the end administered such baptism to the people. Did they stand in the water while he sprinkled or poured it upon them? – this would have been no doubt sufficient. Or did he immerse them completely? – this would have been an even more effective sign of their relinquishing the dying order, and rebirth into the new. We know that he decided to baptise in the Jordan river – the stream on Israel's border that would remind people of the exodus from bondage in Egypt and Israel's entry into the promised land.

John was conscious of the limitations of his ministry compared to the Messiah's. In Malachi's words he was simply the 'messenger' sent to 'prepare the way' – or a mere 'voice' (Mal. 3:1; Isa. 40:3–6). The 'spirit' or 'new heart' would be reserved until the Messiah came to take over. But he would call the remnant forth, and try to match the destroying fire with the fervour of his preaching. If God was really in his heart and mind, the people would hear and come.

It is the first great miracle of the messianic age that the people *did* come! In the hearts of many around the Baptist there had been despair; a willingness to acknowledge that the religious routine of the day, the theology, the empty ceremony, the futile preaching and teaching meant nothing. There had been a hidden hunger for reality, and now here was a man who seemed to be in touch with it. And it is to be noted that they came from miles away to hear him preaching an old-fashioned message, uncritical in its assumptions, and with no relevance to the urgent 'problems of today'.

The Messiah, too, came and took his place among the crowds, for though he had no sin to repent of and confess, he regarded himself as one with those around him. It is remarkable that Jesus was unashamed to stand alongside this enthusiastic charismatic prophet. He acknowledged his greatness, took over, unaltered, his sacrament of baptism, and selected his own first disciples from among his remnant.

THE MESSIAH CHOOSES HIS MISSION AND HIS WAY

In this section we are not attempting to discuss how Jesus found out *who he was* in relation to God, and his distinction from other men, but simply how he found out *what he had to do* to fulfil God's purpose for his life. These two questions should not be confused. If we believe in him we will recognise that to probe the first is quite beyond us, and none of our business anyway. Our concern is with the second.

Not that we doubt who he was. We believe that he was one with God in much more than will and purpose, and therefore different from us in much more than degree and integrity. We will return to a discussion of this later. Meanwhile we concern ourselves with asking how he came to see his messiahship, and how he set about it.

When he was baptised by John their different viewpoints became apparent. John the Baptist had fixed ideas about the Messiah. He expected him to appear before the world in the kingly glory with which the prophets had invested him in their descriptions. With such a Messiah baptism was incompatible. John, recognising who Jesus was, refused to humiliate him: 'I need to be baptised by you, and do you come to me?' (Matt. 3:14).

But Jesus had a fuller picture in his mind. Alongside the messianic king there was the suffering servant – one who would give his back to the smiters, his soul to intercession, his body to be 'led as a lamb to the slaughter' (Isa. 50:6; 53:12). Such had to be his career, and he began it appropriately amidst sinners in the waters of baptism. He had to be 'numbered with the transgressors' whose sin he had come to bear. 'Let it be so,' he said to John, 'for thus it is fitting for us to fulfil *all* righteousness' (Matt. 3:15).

We are told of the vision of the heavens opened, and the voice saying 'This is my beloved Son, with whom I am well pleased.' 'This is my Son' certainly refers to the messianic king described in the second psalm, but 'with whom I am well pleased' comes from one of the poems about the servant in Isaiah (42:1 ff). Heaven, too, affirmed Jesus' choice of career.

Some accounts suggest that John was influenced by Jesus' vision as he came out of the waters of baptism and changed his mind, at least for a while, about the kind of Messiah people must now expect. Shortly after the baptism John pointed Jesus out to his own disciples as 'the Lamb of God who takes away the sin of the world'.[1] But eventually his longing for more evidence of the messianic age than merely a 'lamb led to the slaughter' returned. Even if the Messiah had to offer himself as a sacrifice, John still hankered after visible displays: could the Christ not at least trail a few wispy clouds of glory with him on his way, and prove his person by casting some fire on the dens of corruption? Disappointed, depressed, and lonely, when he was imprisoned by Herod he sent messengers to Jesus asking, 'Are you he who is to come, or look we for another?' Jesus sent back the assuring reply that he was healing and helping many poor people. Were these not true signs that he was the one whom John had expected? John must not be offended that at present there was no more to see.[2]

All his days his baptism was as memorable to Jesus as was the vision that had accompanied it. He never forgot that when he had been baptised by water he had entered a path in which his future destiny was to be baptised again in the same way – but this time cruelly and shamefully by his own blood. Twice it came out in his teaching that this was the way he thought about it. 'I have a baptism to be baptised with,' he once said when speaking on the subject of what the future might hold for himself, 'and how am I constrained until it is accomplished.' And later, as his crucifixion was approaching, he referred to it again as the 'baptism with which I am to be baptised' (Luke 12:50; Mark 10:38).

That he felt 'constrained' from the earliest point in his ministry by his approaching death, foreshadowed in his baptism, comes out again and again in the narrative. For instance, two enigmatic sayings are recorded in the second chapter of Mark's gospel which date very early in his ministry. First of all he forgave the sins of a paralytic man and angered the Pharisees who regarded the gift of forgiveness as the prerogative of God alone. Jesus did not argue with them on this point – it was obviously true! But he added that *even for God* the problem of forgiving sins was greater than any of them imagined it to be. 'Which is easier,' he asked – to say to the paralytic, 'Your sins are forgiven,' or to say, 'Rise, take up your pallet and walk'? The context explains this saying. He is asserting that he *has* the power to forgive only because he himself is on the way to meeting the full cost of forgiveness in the death he has come to achieve (Mark 2:1–12).

Shortly after this incident people challenged him about his laxity, and asked why he did not make his disciples discipline themselves and fast – as John the Baptist had done. His disciples, he answered, would learn the discipline of life in time, as things became harder for them. But, he added, the days of their 'fasting' would come when he would be 'taken away from them' (v. 20).

Later on in his ministry his references to his forthcoming death become more explicit. When Peter confessed him as the 'Christ' at Caesarea Philippi we read that 'from that time Jesus began to show his disciples that he must go to Jerusalem and suffer many things from the elders and chief priests and scribes, and be killed.' It is about this time that he describes his death as not only his future 'baptism' but also as the 'cup' he is going to have to drink – a cup filled with suffering.[3]

There is no suggestion that God communicated directly to Jesus that his will for him was such a self-offering, culminating in violent death. The implication of the narratives is that he found it out first from the Scriptures, especially from the servant prophecies which are often quoted, and as he set out on the way dictated by what was written, divine confirmation was given to him in such theophanies as took place at his baptism and transfiguration, and in other occasional experiences (Matt. 3:16; 17:1 ff; John 12:28, etc). The way he found guidance about what he must do is summed up in his own saying, 'The Son of man goes as it is written of him.'[4] Time and again on his way to the cross we find him conforming his activity to the details of the prophecies about the Messiah. John the evangelist was so impressed by this aspect of his career that he interrupts his passion narrative several times with the comment, 'This was to fulfil the Scripture.'[5]

THE CROSS AS THE EXPRESSION AND MEANS OF SELF-GIVING LOVE

We often speak of the negative consequences of Christ's death – he went to the cross to save us from the dire consequences of our sin. But it is brought out clearly in the Gospels that he also had a more positive aim: he died so that he might impart what he had to each and every one of us. He stressed this aspect of his death at the Last Supper, when he gave his disciples a symbol of his death. Having blessed the bread and identified it with himself ('this is my body') 'he broke' it. His death gives us everything he himself has. When he spoke about his being the 'bread of life' by the eating of which we would 'live for ever', he was saying the same thing: this 'eating' becomes possible only through his death. He spoke of his flesh as being given in his death not simply to be *sacrificed* for the life of the world, but to be *partaken* of, that the world might live (cf. Mark 14:22; John 6:51). His death on the cross was simply a final act of self-giving that had its roots early in his human life.

Jesus is portrayed in the Gospels as one who, even amidst suffering, and though always under the shadow of his cross, experienced all the 'blessedness' he spoke of in the Beatitudes. He often showed a consciousness of the presence of God quite unique to his own person; he was inspired by a clear vision of God, and enjoyed a pure spontaneous freedom before God, an unshakeable certainty in his sonship to God, and a peace and joy which he knew and spoke of as peculiarly his own. He was born with this, and grew up with it. Only sin could have spoiled it, and he had none.[6]

He was also acutely aware that around him, men and women with their vitiated personal relationships, their uncontrolled lusts, their petty, tragic follies, their love of power and money, seemed to have forfeited what he himself possessed. No one else shared the 'blessedness' which he had. He referred to this constantly in his teaching. A gulf appeared to separate him from all others. He alone was right, all others erred. He alone was the true light, all others were engulfed in darkness. He alone knew who he was and where he was going, all others were lost. He alone understood and enjoyed true health, all others were sick. He alone was strong, all others faltered.

But his consciousness of being so different did not set him apart from others; rather, precisely because of this difference, he drew closer to them.[7] It was surely with growing feelings of horror and pity that he observed what was going on in the minds and hearts of those around him, and was stirred into action. His impulse was always to give what he had. And this same self-giving impulse, this love, led to his ultimate sacrifice of himself on Calvary. If he alone knew the way, then he must show it to all others and be the good shepherd, even though it meant laying down his life. If he alone was right before God and had special access to God, then he had to use this to plead mercy for all others. If he alone had health and the power to heal, he must become the physician of all the sick around him. If he alone had satisfaction and joy in God, he must become the 'bread for the life of the world'.

From the moment of his baptism, to share, and to give himself without limit or restraint, was the passion behind all his teaching, praying, and miracle-working. Always he was the one who possessed everything seeking to share with a world that lacked everything, and when those around him imagined they did not need what he sought to give them, he pitied and grieved for them. The effort constantly exhausted him, and his resources had to be continually renewed in prayer.[8] He lived and was inspired by the Spirit of God.

He discovered as time went on that his contacts with those to whom he brought forgiveness, healing, and new life in God, brought upon himself a deepening share of the human suffering he was trying to banish. We have to note what the evangelists say, in their sometimes allegorical way, when they tell us that Jesus 'touched' those he healed. Matthew, after recounting the healing of Peter's mother-in-law by touch, tells us briefly of more healings by the word and then adds: 'This was to fulfil what was spoken by the prophet Isaiah, "He took our infirmities, and bore our diseases" ' (Matt. 8:14–17). In giving, he has to *take*. Does this not imply that he was able to impart healing through the word only because he took on himself something of the weakness and disease he was banishing, and that his laying his hand on those who were being healed was a sign of a two-way giving and receiving? Luke records his touching of the leper in a significant scene of contrast between the healed man being sent to the temple for his certificate of cleansing, and Jesus the healer going apart into the wilderness – the place into which those with leprosy were banished.[9]

This active participation in the suffering of those around him, and the scorn poured on him by those who misunderstood and rejected his advances, made up for him a burden of agony from which he sought release in his prayers for help to God, for himself as well as for those around him – for he began to feel that his own life must be at stake if the life of any around him remained at stake. 'In the days of his flesh, Jesus offered up prayers and supplications with loud cries and tears, to him who was able to save him from death.' It was such a prayer, beginning when he began his ministry, that found its climax in Gethsemane when 'being in an agony he prayed more earnestly' (Heb. 5:7; Luke 22:44).

THE WAY OF ATONEMENT AS THE WAY OF SACRIFICE

It was more than a desire to share that took Jesus to the cross. It was a desire to save. Those around him were not only deprived, but threatened. They were under guilt before God and bondage to evil. An act of expiation and redemption was needed to save them from both aspects of their plight. In our next section we will discuss how Jesus concerned himself about their bondage. Here we discuss how he concerned himself about their guilt.

When he healed the paralytic man he made it clear that in his ministry forgiveness of sins was much more important than the healing of the body,[10] and his earnestness to demonstrate that he had the power to forgive sins while he was on earth is striking. Undoubtedly the disciples were drawn to him all the more because they experienced his forgiving love and power as equivalent to the forgiving love and power of God himself (Mark 2:10; Luke 7:47–50; 5:8–10).

There is little doubt that as his death approached he saw himself as soon purposively to become involved in the consequences of human sin. A. M. Hunter points out that the 'cup' he spoke of, which he must drink, could be interpreted, from the servant songs of Isaiah, as the cup of God' anger – a cup not simply of divinely appointed suffering but also of divinely appointed punishment. It was with thoughts of such a cup of punishment that he shrank from his death in the Garden of Gethsemane (Luke 22:42). He saw himself as dying to offer himself as a sacrifice for the sins of others. Revealing his thoughts on this, he said, 'The Son of man also came not to be served but to serve, and to give his life as a ransom for many.' The word 'many' refers to the servant of the Lord in Isaiah who was to bear the sin of 'many' by his submission to suffering and his intercession. The idea of his 'giving his life as a ransom' probably refers to the expiatory gift by which a price was paid as a substitute penalty to save a guilty man's life. The preposition used in the phrase 'for many' could be read 'in place of many' – again stressing the idea of his offering himself in place of others as a sacrifice (Mark 10:45; Isa. 53:12; Exod. 21:30).

It should be noted that in most of the sayings in which Jesus speaks of his death, he refers to himself as 'the Son of man'. The 'Son of man' is the glorious figure in human form in Daniel 7, who at the end of all the ages comes embodying in himself the people of God, to rule in place of the cruel beasts who have hitherto had dominion on the earth. Therefore Jesus regarded himself as the one who at the end includes in himself, or merges into, the 'remnant' or the 'saints of the Most High'. In using the term 'the Son of man' so frequently when speaking of what he had to accomplish in his death, Jesus was also saying: This is indeed the way I enter into and reveal my glory!

Jesus' words at the Last Supper about the cup are also revealing. Matthew gives the fullest record. 'This is my blood of the covenant which is poured out for many for the forgiveness of sins.' The words take us back to Jeremiah's description of the new covenant (the Marcan version, for example, refers to it as 'the blood of the new covenant') which the Messiah has to inaugurate, when sin is to be forgiven by a miracle of grace and the law written on the hearts of God's people. They refer also to the ratification of the covenant at Sinai with the sacrificial blood of an animal which was sprinkled over the book and the representatives of the people, enabling them to 'eat and drink and see God'. They also refer to the blood of the original passover feast which, after slaying the sacrificial animal, was sprinkled on the lintels and doorposts of the houses of those who were to be saved in the coming exodus. And they take us back once again to Isaiah 53, with the reference to 'many', and to other servant songs which tell of the servant as given for a covenant (Matt. 26:28; Jer. 31:31 ff; Exod. 12:7; Exod. 24; Isa. 42:6; 49:8).

Jesus, with all this in mind, was saying that his own life, by being poured out in his death as a sacrifice, was going to effect all the promises of forgiveness and new life in Jeremiah's vision. He was also declaring that just as Moses, with the blood of the old covenant, led the old exodus from the bondage of Egypt, so he, the mediator of the new covenant, by his *own* blood, was going to lead his people in a new exodus out of bondage to sin and guilt into the new age of freedom before God.

We have already noted that many aspects of the meaning of the Old Testament sacrificial rituals and ceremonies were hidden from the participants. In linking his death so precisely with the old rites regarding the shedding of blood, Jesus was indicating that the true hidden meaning of these rites was now to be sought in what he was going to do in his own death, and was to be understood from this point of view. What Moses and the prophets could only grope after, Jesus' disciples were now to begin to understand – and yet how little they were to understand, for they and all others are finally excluded from the holy of holies into which he, the great high priest, enters alone!

The accounts of the Last Supper indicate that Jesus deliberately abstained from taking the cup himself. Indeed, he uttered what is sometimes described as a 'vow of abstinence'. Referring to the feast (which was meant to be a feast of liberation), he said: 'I shall not eat it, until it is fulfilled in the kingdom of God.' Referring to the cup (which undoubtedly symbolised in this case joy and privilege), he said, 'Take this and divide it among yourselves; for I tell you that from now on I shall not drink of the fruit of the vine until the kingdom of God comes' (Luke 22:15–18). It is quite clear that they drink the cup of joy (wine) because he abstains, and drinks the cup of wrath and judgment. They will never experience that judgment. No one could have borne it except he, and he will bear it all, not only for them but for all. They can now feast because he sorrows. They can live because he dies.

The accounts insist that he agonised alone. Inevitably the disciples stayed uncomprehending and at a distance, sleeping, when he took them into Gethsemane. He went alone to the cross and we hear the cry 'My God, my God, why hast thou forsaken me' (Matt. 27:46). When we try to interpret these words we become so convinced of the superficiality of our deepest thoughts that we have to admit that we, too, are standing, uncomprehending, a great way off. We find ourselves led to the realisation that at this point the sufferings of Jesus which we have tried to understand as far as we can through the human analogies available to us, take on an intensity beyond our imagination and also a quality we are incapable of defining. The analogies we have used so far take us only to a threshold. What happened beyond this, the crucial element in his cross, gives his atoning act its glory, and its redeeming power.

THE WAY OF ATONEMENT AS THE WAY OF CONFLICT

At his baptism Jesus consecrated himself to make his life a living sacrifice and at the same time to engage in a relentless, continual and ultimately decisive conflict with evil powers which he knew to dominate this world's life and to effect human misery, corruption, decay and death.[11] The Gospel writers emphasise that under the power of the Spirit, he immediately plunged himself into this conflict: 'Then was Jesus led up by the Spirit into the wilderness to be tempted by the devil.' It is significant that, according to Luke, for example, shortly after his decisive first victory over the devil, the onlookers were 'amazed' at the intentness and effectiveness of his attacks on the evil spirits which he saw distorting and hampering the health and freedom of men and women around him. 'For with authority and power he commands the unclean spirits and they come out.' Casting out demons was linked in his mind with curing all other varieties of sickness, as 'destroying the works of the devil'. Jesus regarded his extraordinary success in both types of miracle as a sign that the new messianic age in which all these things were foretold, had indeed begun to happen. 'If I by the Spirit of God cast out devils then is the kingdom of God come upon you' (Luke 4:36; 1 John 3:8; Matt. 12:28).

But of what use simply to cancel out, here and there, the evil works of Satan, without destroying the evil one himself? 'How can one enter a strong man's house and plunder his goods, unless he first binds the strong man?' Therefore Jesus regarded these miracles as mere preliminary skirmishes in an ongoing guerrilla operation which could only be fruitful if it led up to a final decisive battle with the entrenched forces of the establishment. Satan himself is regarded as retreating into guerrilla tactics after a first shock defeat when Jesus overcame him in the temptation. Luke says he 'departed from Jesus till an opportune time.' This is better translated as in the Jerusalem Bible 'to return at the appointed time'. The 'appointed time' was of course the day of the final conflict which Jesus had come to enter (Matt. 12:29; Luke 4:13, cf. NEB, 'biding his time'). All his life Jesus deliberately moved towards such a decisive battle, clearing the ground of the petty hindrances put in his way by the establishment of the day behind which the evil power was covering up a lurking retreat.

In Jesus' mind Satan was doomed from the start. He knew himself as the 'strong' Redeemer, and described himself as the 'stronger one' in the conflict. When his mission of preaching and healing went well he regarded it as a foretaste of the final triumph. When the disciples reported their successes to him, he rejoiced and said, 'I saw Satan fall like lightning from heaven' (Luke 11:22; 10:18).

Yet right from the start this war and his victories cost him a protracted and great sacrifice of himself. Agonising toil and prayer were to him the price of the freedom he was seeking for others. Conflict with the powers of evil also cost Jesus the virulent hatred of the ruling authorities of his nation, their continual persecution, and ultimately his death. We have to be careful in our interpretation of Jesus' conflict with the authorities and with the 'law' in his day. He had no desire to attack the 'establishment' as such. He was not a revolutionary and he always inculcated respect for lawful authority (Matt. 23:2; 17:27; 22:21). But the powers of evil which he was attacking entrenched themselves in the authorities who faced Jesus, and those rulers were to blame for leaving themselves open to such evil influence. Under it they distorted his teaching, persecuted those he healed, put obstacles in his way at every step, and finally killed him.[12]

In the Gospel of John the time of his final conflict with Satan, and the conflict itself, are referred to as Jesus' 'hour'. It is mentioned three times, early in the ministry, as having 'not yet come'. To Jesus it was the hour when the 'ruler of this world' was to be 'cast out', and when he himself was to be glorified. But far from being an hour of triumph and unmixed glory it was to him the hour of intense shame, disgust and horror. He summed up his dread of the coming conflict when he spoke of 'the power of darkness', for in some strange way, to rescue us from our evil he had to submit himself to the worst tortures of close encounter with evil. This is why at Gethsemane he prayed to be spared from some of the vicissitudes of the battle he was entering. He shrank then from the 'hour' as from the 'cup' (John 2:4; 7:30; 8:20; 12:23, 27; Luke 22:53).

No doubt he called his final conflict the 'hour' to emphasise the special viciousness of the attack by the power of evil; the conflict had attained a particular intensity that marked it off from all the previous events of his life. The fact, too, that he entered this last battle already wearied with toil, and physically broken, called for the more desperate effort of all his already exhausted strength, and added to his agony.

As Jesus entered Jerusalem on Palm Sunday to set the stage for his final conflict, we know that he had in mind a passage from Zechariah 9, from which the text comes, 'Behold, your king is coming to you, humble and mounted upon an ass.' The context of this passage reveals a clue to the thoughts that went through Jesus' mind as he approached his death. The verses following the quotation above read:

> As for you also, because of the blood of my covenant with you, I will set your captives free from the waterless pit. Return to your stronghold, O prisoners of hope . . .

Here the 'blood' is obviously not *only* the blood of the covenant sacrifice, but also the blood of the warrior who has come to set prisoners free, whose garments are blood-soaked because it has been indeed for him a 'bloody' and bitter affray. Yet the captives go free with only his blood shed (Matt. 21:5, cf. Zech. 9:9, 11–12).

The thought of this passage is re-echoed in the book of Revelation when John sees the warrior on the white horse who is the Word of God coming in his final triumphant procession to establish the kingdom. He is followed by the armies of heaven 'arrayed in fine linen white and pure', mounted on white horses. But there is no battle nor even one to come. Armies arrayed in such spotless dress do not go to battle. The battle has already been fought and won by the one on the white horse, and his clothes alone bear the marks.[13]

3 The apostolic understanding of the cross

Most of this section is devoted to the meaning given to Christ's death in the Pauline Epistles. A convenient way of arranging the material is to discuss first the terms Paul uses to describe what Christ has achieved for us through his death, and then to consider his thought as to how such a death has brought about this achievement. We are, of course, covering much of the same ground as in our first section, but we hope to find that the use of different language and imagery gives us a better grasp of what has already been said, and clarifies some of the implications of what we are trying to understand.

We shall discuss the terms used in the Epistles to describe Christ's work: reconciliation, justification, sanctification, salvation, redemption, regeneration, new creation, revelation. These are not all peculiarly Pauline words. 'Revelation' occurs here and there in the New Testament. 'Regeneration' is used by Jesus in the Gospels, and an equivalent term 'the restoration of all things' is used in Acts. So too with the words 'salvation' and 'redemption'. But Paul uses these words in such a way that more easily than in other contexts we are able to see them closely related to the work of Christ.

The writers of the New Testament did not use words idly. Different words were deliberately chosen to bring out distinct aspects of what Christ has done. We cannot fully understand what they were saying unless we try to interpret precisely what these words meant within the contexts in which they were used. However this does not mean that when we preach what we have understood from the New Testament we are at liberty, or even that it is desirable, to use other words and imagery, or to coin new words. It is erroneous to think that we can understand these words by substituting for them so-called synonyms that are easier to understand. It is often suggested today that we can substitute for the word 'justification' the word 'acceptance'. But Paul knew this word too and used it seldom, because 'justification' had a more complex meaning. So also 'forgiveness' means slightly less than Paul intended when he used 'reconciliation'.

The terms we have chosen are used in the New Testament with a double reference. They stand each for something that has taken place for all men (and indeed to some extent apart from all men) in and through the work of Christ in his life, death and resurrection – something we could call 'objective' or 'cosmic' in its reference and implications. But they also stand for something that is uniquely individual, intimate and subjective; a happening or effect within the mind and heart, or a word or opportunity offered to the mind and heart of each single person. Thus reconciliation, as we shall see, is something God has already done for the world before any appeal to accept it reaches the individual. Our sanctification is something perfectly worked out for each of us – as well as for all – in the sanctification Christ perfected for himself on the cross, and then secondly something we take each to ourselves by 'putting on' Christ. 'Regeneration' refers first of all to the whole new world, the dawning age of 'all things . . . made new', which God has already brought into being for the sake of Christ, and which is simply manifesting itself in fresh signs when the Spirit makes each of us the new creatures we become in Christ. 'Justification' is first something done by God for Christ, and by Christ for God, and by both for all mankind, before it ever becomes our own justification by faith in Christ. Our thinking about the atonement is most fruitful when we keep clearly distinct in our minds its aspect as an objective work before we confuse this with what happens within ourselves.

In our study of the mind and purpose of Jesus we noted that his conflict almost merged into his sacrifice to become one and the same thing, and yet it was an important and distinct aspect in itself. So the meanings of our chosen words merge into one another. Words like 'salvation', 'regeneration' and 'redemption' indeed overlap so much that we have to treat them all together. The chief difference between them is that they indicate how Christ meets different aspects of our human need.

THE ATONEMENT AS AN ACT OF RECONCILIATION

We begin with Paul's statement of the atonement as an act of reconciliation in 2 Corinthians:

> Therefore, if any one is in Christ, he is a new creation; the old has passed away, behold, the new has come. All this is from God, who through Christ reconciled us to himself and gave us the ministry of reconciliation; that is, God was in Christ reconciling the world to himself, not counting their trespasses against them, and entrusting to us the message of reconciliation. So we are ambassadors for Christ,

33

God making his appeal through us. We beseech you on behalf of Christ, be reconciled to God. For our sake he made him to be sin who knew no sin, so that in him we might become the righteousness of God (2 Cor. 5:17–21).

Here Paul is making a very simple appeal to us to become reconciled to God – reinforced by theological considerations which we can easily appreciate. But at the same time he shows that the appeal, and our response, are possible only because of a reconciling act of God as wonderful as a new creation, and infinite in its cost.

Be reconciled

Superficially these words seem to define simply the plight we are in and its remedy. There has been a tragic and hurtful breach between us and God. Paul in other places calls it 'alienation' or 'enmity' (e.g. Col. 1:21). The most common Old Testament analogy for such alienation of mind and heart between persons is that of God's bride leaving him to become a harlot (Hos. 1:1–2; Jer. 2:32,37). But Paul no doubt had in mind Jesus' analogy of the son who has become the prodigal in a far country. Our sin is mistrust of the Father's love, a pride that wills to be independent and aloof, though at the same time we may be squandering his bounty. It shows itself around us today time and again in the inexplicable hatred for good parents that can so easily possess children (and sometimes vice versa), and that tends always to harden beyond the possibility of response to any loving appeal. Sadly, love can burn the more on the other side, the more it is rejected.

What does reconciliation mean, since we are caught in such an attitude to God? It means that, like the prodigal, we must be made to think again about the true family life of God, to which we should belong, and about what God is really like. It means that a miracle must happen to us as happened in Jesus' parable of the prodigal son when he 'came to himself'. Indeed, ours must be the miracle of a 'new creation' – the kind Jesus performed when he raised a dead son from his coffin and 'restored him to his mother' – as a parable of the greater works he was later to do when he rose again (Luke 7:15). All this is what God has to do for us in reconciling us, but on our part reconciliation means a willingness to turn and change – for ever – and return home. And when we receive the reconciliation we know that we are back, accepted not grudgingly but lovingly with open arms, and given not only a meal at the table, but a seat at the hearth.

If any one is in Christ

'Be reconciled' in our text is exactly synonymous to 'be in Christ', and one phrase follows the other interchangeably. Usually 'be in Christ' describes the deep and intensely personal relationship of faith that is set up between a new believer and the risen Christ. Signs of this new and creative personal union are baptism, participation in the Lord's Supper, membership of the Christian community. Often evidence is given of its reality and power in remarkable changes in outlook and way of life – the *new creation* in which *the old is passed away*.

God . . . through Christ reconciled . . . the world to himself

These particular words bring out an important aspect of the whole passage. Paul emphasises that the reconciliation has already taken place in the humanity of Jesus Christ before it affects us. When Christ offered himself to God, all his life and finally on the cross in our name and place, he was not only our substitute, he was also our representative, and indeed the representative of all mankind. In the Epistle to the Colossians Paul speaks of our having been reconciled to God in Christ in order that we might be *presented* to God in Christ 'holy, blameless and irreproachable before him' (1:22). The thought of reconciliation seems to flow easily into, first, the thought of our representation in Christ, and then the thought of our self-presentation in Christ to God.

In his act of 'presenting' us to God in his humanity, what Christ offered God in our name was a full response of reconciliation adequate in every respect. It was the kind of response we ourselves as truly penitent sinners would have made should the possibility ever have come our way. It was a returning home; a confession in our name that we have been without excuse and wholly in the wrong; a vow on our behalf that we will live for ever in the presence of the Father. Christ has given all this in our name, and has given a pledge in his own name that no one coming through him would ever be allowed to fall back.

This full and adequate response of reconciliation to God's love is perfectly described for us in the parable of the prodigal son, from the moment that 'he came to himself' and said, 'I will arise and go to my father' (Luke 15:17–18). If the parable suggests to us that we ourselves can achieve such a 'coming to ourselves' – a repentant heart, new thoughts of God, and finding the way home – it dares to suggest this only because Christ has already done it for us, in our name, and in our place.[1] When we ourselves come to be 'in Christ', then all that he has already done for us in reconciling us to the Father is realised within us, and we find ourselves through the Spirit of sonship which we receive from Christ, yielding ourselves back to God in love, repeating earnestly in our hearts the prayer of pleading, confidence and sonship that he took up for us on the cross. Thus we are brought through Jesus to the Father. He is, as Augustine remarked, the way by which we go as well as the truth to which we come.

God was in Christ

In our passage God is the subject of the verb 'to reconcile'. It is we who are reconciled. Some of the forms of the Greek verb Paul uses for 'reconcile' are used in current religious thought with God as object, and imply man's action on God who is somehow propitiated and made forgiving. Paul deliberately avoids this use of the verb and selects one that can imply simply something that God does graciously, on his own initiative, on behalf of man.[2]

Paul explicitly mentions here God's coming to us in Christ, but behind his coming there lie (and Paul has these in mind too) the costly acts of God turning to us and giving himself to us in his own mind and heart. In Christ God turns to man before man turns to God. God reconciles himself to man before he reconciles man to himself. The Old Testament, as we have indicated already, has many pictures of God dealing with himself before dealing with men. We are shown God perplexed, baffled, agonising, weighing his own reaction to our human sin before expressing his love and righteousness in his dealings with his people. The New Testament does not show us this inner aspect of the life of God. It assumes that we know it because we have the same God in Christ as he who dealt with Israel. But if God 'did not spare himself' (Rom. 8:32) in yielding his Son, neither did he spare himself in deciding to turn towards us in the first place.

Him he made to be sin

Three or four times we are reminded in the passage that 'reconciliation' as we have described it is only one aspect of what took place in Christ. The stress in the passage on the 'new creation' reminds us that to be reconciled involves for us a change not merely in our disposition but in 'our total state of life'.[3] Paul speaks in Colossians of God as designing in Christ to 'reconcile to himself all things, whether on earth or in heaven'.

The mention that God does not impute to us our trespasses leads our thought into the doctrine of justification. The last sentence of our passage reminds us that being reconciled involves both Christ and ourselves in making an exchange.[4] Christ, in reconciling us to the Father, took our sins upon himself so completely that Paul describes him as being 'made sin'. Surely this again hints at the damnation or dereliction that was reserved to come upon him not in the course of his life but at the very end. It is Paul's way of reminding us of the crucial 'hour' on the cross when he drank the cup, and faced the power of darkness. But if he took our sins upon himself in this way, then exactly in this way he offers to us his righteousness. This is no fiction, no mere act of stopping at 'non-imputation' of guilt – though this, thank God, is involved too. This righteousness is our possession as surely as Christ himself is our possession. It can grow within us as our relationship with Christ can grow. It is the beginning of the new creation.

THE ATONEMENT AS AN ACT OF JUSTIFICATION

In the alienation that has taken place between ourselves and God we have lost more than our home and the friendship which truly fulfils our life. We have also lost our right-standing. We can no longer be counted reliable and trustworthy before the only tribunal that matters. Sin has brought about a moral crisis as well as a personal one. There is not only love in the world which we have forsaken and to which we seek to return in reconciliation, but also a law which encloses love. The God to whom we seek to return is one whose love expresses itself in ways that are constant and upon which trust can be built. He seeks and expects loyalty. His forgiveness means our restoration to a covenant relationship which demands and inspires uprightness and reliability. What we require from God, then, when we return to him, is not simply a welcome and a seat at the hearth, but a declaration of our right-standing in his eyes. We need to know that we are counted upon as capable of starting again and of going straight ahead, unhampered by the past we have lived.

God our Father controls all life and does business. He has a realm and a universe as well as a home. He keeps the law of the world going as well as the love of the world. Paul encourages us to imagine that he has a courthouse within his realm and that for our return he settles our affairs there as well as within the home. He is prepared to work miracles with the computer that records our past as with the forces that shape our present and our future. The apostle therefore speaks of our receiving justification through Christ as well as reconciliation. This means more than pardon: 'It means winning or being granted a position of acceptance.'[5] To secure such a 'position of acceptance' involves a justifying action in God's court in which our past in all its details is condemned and its consequences are fully covered, yet the verdict that we should be accepted is totally vindicated.[6] As C. K. Barrett points out, reconciliation and justification are very close together. 'Reconciliation is located in God's court, and, expressed in forensic terms, means justification.'[7] Yet they are quite distinct. The strong and free righteousness with which God assures us that our past is forgiven and guarantees our future, supplements the kindling love which reconciles us to his heart.

An important passage from Romans 3 illustrates Paul's thought on the atonement as an act of justification:

> But now the righteousness of God has been manifested apart from the law, although the law and the prophets bear witness to it, the righteousness of God through faith in Jesus Christ for all who believe. For there is no distinction; since all have sinned and fall short of the glory of God, they are justified by his grace as a gift, through the redemption which is in Christ Jesus, whom God put forward as an expiation by his blood, to be received by faith. This was to show God's righteousness, because in his divine forbearance he had passed over former sins; it was to prove at the present time that he himself is righteous, and that he justifies him who has faith in Jesus (Rom. 3:21–6).

Several important features of Paul's thought stand out clearly.

History and the righteousness of God

All through past ages God's righteousness has been called in question everywhere on earth because of the forbearance with which he has treated human sin. Never has it been judged, punished, crushed as it should have been. Paul in his speech to the Athenians summed up God's attitude to sin hitherto with the words: 'The times of disobedience God winked at.' It is true that the Old Testament relates the grim fearful judgments with which God at times visited many nations, especially his own people. But such judgments were always restrained, and are called only a 'little wrath'. On the whole, history has shown that far too often evil men profit well by their evil ways. If in this context God simply justified all the ungodly without doing something about his reputation for past laxity, would his action not simply encourage the world in its carelessness to truth, honour and right? (cf. Acts 17:30, AV; Hos. 11:9; Isa. 54:7).

The cross and the righteousness of God

In justifying the ungodly in Christ, God has vindicated his righteousness once-for-all. The death of his Son is an act of expiation, fearful in the implications of its necessity, and costly and bitter in its fulfilment. No one with the least understanding of this cost and its meaning can ever regard sin as trifling, or God's righteousness as something overcast with a doubtful shadow. In Jesus' death God visited human sin with all the judgment it deserves. And Jesus in accepting the cross affirmed such a sentence. In the cross God, from the very throne of heaven, as it were, declared himself righteous in his justification of those who believe in Jesus.

Moreover, in Christ's death God not only manifested and upheld what we might call his 'legal' or 'self-vindicating' righteousness as the upholder of law, order and stability in the universe, he also sought to impart his righteousness as a saving gift to the ungodly who trust in his promises and his covenant. In the Old Testament the 'righteousness of God' is often appealed to by the poor and needy, and it is used by God to liberate the oppressed. God brings or communicates it to those who seek him and hunger and thirst for such a gift.[8] To be justified through the cross is to be justified 'by his grace, freely'. Such grace does not need to be made propitious before it flows, along with righteousness, to the ungodly.

The cross as the place where sin is dealt with

Anyone who reads the various best-known translations of the first half of v. 25 will be perplexed. The Authorised Version says, 'whom God set forth *as a propitiation* through faith in his blood'. Most of the modern versions change the central word to *expiation*. But the Jerusalem Bible says simply that Christ 'was appointed by God to sacrifice his life to win reconciliation.' James Denney suggests the phrase 'as of propitiatory value'. The word causing so much difficulty is *hilastērion*, a Greek word which could literally also mean the 'mercy seat' of the ark in the temple. Hence we are justified in assuming that the death of Jesus is treated here as a sacrifice and the cross is regarded as the place where sin is dealt with as in the temple.

A further question at issue in this discussion on the meaning of the text is whether Paul had in mind the idea of Christ's death being a means of meeting or allaying the anger of God, or of dealing with it so that it will no longer fall on those for whom the sacrifice is made. In this case the word propitiation would be the most suitable. Expiation implies simply that God has done away with sin itself.

We have already suggested that the Old Testament sacrifices were generally regarded as expiating sin rather than as propitiating God (see p. 3). But the New Testament use of a word is not entirely decided by the Old Testament, and the case for using propitiation here can be strongly supported by the fact that the context in which the passage occurs speaks much of the 'wrath of God'. Yet Paul, when he uses the phrase, is referring to justification and justice, and in this more immediate context we would tend to think of Christ as suffering a penalty for sin rather than the 'wrath of God'. Judges are unprofessional if they give place to anger.

Of course, Christ in his cross does in some way deal with the 'wrath of God'. But Paul uses this in connection with his work of salvation, and we will discuss it under the latter heading.

The inner meaning of expiation

The passage before us brings out most clearly that what Christ bore on Calvary was the penalty for human sin. He expiated our sin by receiving in himself its judicial consequences. What happened to him was an act of judgment in which all our sin, having been totally condemned, was punished and put away. Thus it was dealt with righteously. It was with this in mind that Paul later in the same letter could put the good news so confidently: 'There is therefore now no condemnation for those who are in Christ Jesus' (Rom. 8:1).

THE ATONEMENT AS AN ACT OF REDEMPTION

In the Old Testament, sin is shown to be always at work in an endless variety of forms, enslaving and destroying. In the form of idolatry it dominated the life of the people of God from generation to generation, corrupted every aspect of their moral life, and robbed God of their service. In the form of perverted sex it made the city of Sodom a place of unspeakable cruelty, oppression and depravity. In the form of greed it constantly caught up the rich into a financial manipulation and social ordering of affairs that crushed and deprived the poor even of their means of livelihood. In its manifestly brutal forms it brought all the atrocities of war. In the lives of individuals, too, sin was always ready to take over, with devastating effects. Ahab, well intentioned at first, was finally a destroyer of truth and goodness in his land; David gave way to lust and sowed the seeds of bitter tragedy for all his growing family.

These stories formed the background of Paul's thinking. He obviously never forgot the comment of the Old Testament writer on Ahab, that he 'sold himself to do evil in the sight of the Lord'. The power to which he sold himself was simply that of an evil personal force stronger than himself and determined to pervert him in every way (1 Kings 22:25).

Paul described his own state, in common with other men, as being 'sold under sin'. And he called what he shared with all men, the general instability and weakness of his natural human make-up, the 'flesh', and he recognised that in his 'flesh', i.e., what he was by nature, 'sin' had made its home. He spoke often of sin 'dwelling in my flesh' or 'in me'. He found that sin could reign in every aspect of his life (Rom. 7:4, 17–18, 20). Early in his life, in the form of pride, morality and religion, it had alienated him entirely from God and made him the vicious enemy of the truth and goodness that were in Christ, and a murderer of his people.

In his analysis of what has gone wrong with humanity he did not hesitate to name other enemies who held people in bondage. Besides 'sin' there was the devil and 'death'. From his own experience of contemporary life he could also name the 'law' as belonging to the same company. When he spoke of these 'enemies' he seems to have conceived of them not as abstract entities but as half-personal realities, demonic powers capable of deceiving men and tyrannising them; bringing them 'the more they yielded, into ever deepening bondage, indeed into the realm of utter despair'.[9]

It was against this background that Paul spoke about the atonement as the 'liberating act' or 'redemption which is in Christ Jesus'.[10]

The curse of the law

Paul saw that when Jesus came to deliver mankind from the power of sin, the most sinister aspects of our human bondage and of the workings of evil were shown up vividly. Those in authority at the time who most actively engineered the crucifixion did so in the name of the 'law', which in their tradition was as holy as the temple and the name of God himself. They saw Jesus as threatening the core of their religious life. He had proclaimed himself superior to the tradition they believed came unchanged and unchangeable from God through Moses. No doubt they persuaded Judas that he was doing a noble work in upholding the law when he betrayed his friend. 'We have a law,' they said, 'and by our law he ought to perish.'[11]

Paul saw clearly that the powers of the day who crucified the Redeemer not only covered what they did with the cloak of the law, but also found in the law the inspiration for their action. From his observations Paul discovered one of the great original insights into the Christian faith. This was that the powers of evil in extending their bondage over humanity entrenched themselves behind the law, and were able to do their worst work from this position. 'The power of sin is in the law,' he wrote (1 Cor. 15:56). Moreover, the powers of evil turned the law into one of the greatest potential enemies of what was Christian.

Looking back on his own past life Paul had to admit that he had found it so. During his early career, when his life and heart were so alienated from God, the law and his love for the law had kept him far from God. The law had promised life to him: believing in it, he had wanted to do what was right. Even when he had experienced failure, by abiding by it he had felt that ultimately his course was right.

Looking back on the history of the nation, he began to see a long-established connection between sin and the law. Sin was certainly in the world before the law was given by Moses, but when the law came it seemed to multiply as if provoked. As V. P. Furnish observes, if the flesh was 'sin's host' the law was 'sin's agent'. It 'worked wrath'.[12]

Originally the law was given for a good purpose. It was God's gift to his people. It revealed his will and something of his nature. A summary of it, in the ten commandments, was enclosed in the ark of the covenant in the temple. It was there to help to maintain both a proper distance and true communion between God and his people. It could inspire fear in those who believed in God, and restrain their lawless tendencies. In itself it was beneficial and holy (Rom. 7:13, 16).

The law brought a twofold curse on those under it – both because of its goodness and in spite of its goodness. It brought a curse on those who failed to keep it, and terrified them. It brought a more dreadful curse on those who made it their refuge from God, and became the servants of the evil they found entrenched there.

Redemption from the curse of the law

Paul spoke about this aspect of the work of Christ especially in his letter to the Galatians. For the Galatian Christians, after starting out well, putting their trust in Christ and Christ alone for salvation, had begun to think that they could make great progress in the Christian way if they put some trust in legal achievements and legal observances. In two short passages Paul, to put them right, referred them back to Christ's work on the cross effecting redemption from the curse of the law:

> Christ redeemed us from the curse of the law, having become a curse for us – for it is written, 'Cursed be every one who hangs on a tree' – that in Christ Jesus the blessing of Abraham might come upon the Gentiles, that we might receive the promise of the Spirit through faith (Gal. 3:13–14).

> So with us; when we were children, we were slaves to the elemental spirits of the universe. But when the time had fully come, God sent forth his Son, born of woman, born under the law, to redeem those who were under the law, so that we might receive adoption as sons (Gal. 4:3–6).

We must look at both passages together to grasp Paul's meaning. Jesus, born under the law like everyone else, was different in that he kept to the law – yet different also in that he alone suffered its full curse.[13] No one should have escaped its curse except he alone – and he alone took it. This is our liberation from the penalty of the law. Because it fell on him it does not fall on us. We are also delivered from the power of the accusations of the law to terrify us. Because it accused and penalised Jesus, the law has proved itself a false, mistaken accuser. By taking on himself the curse of the law, Jesus 'as an innocent person has nullified completely the indicting power of the law'.[14]

Both texts describe Christ as effecting between us and himself an exchange of status and condition. *We* were *slaves* but now we have received the *adoption* of *sons*. *He* was the *Son* and free, but he accepted *slavery* under the law which bound us. *He* took the *curse* so that *we* and all men might enjoy the *blessing*.

Another important feature of Paul's thought is to be found in the way he links up the death of Christ directly with his birth. For Christ, to accept birth among us was to accept the cross. The shadow of Calvary falls over the cradle of the Christ child.

The defeat of the 'principalities and powers'

In robbing the law of its power to condemn, Christ settled the fate of the alien powers entrenched within it. Paul writes:

God . . . cancelled the bond which stood against us with its legal demands; this he set aside, nailing it to the cross. He disarmed the principalities and powers and made a public example of them, triumphing over them in him (Col. 2:14–15).

Paul is very obscure here, probably he is talking chiefly about the wisdom of God, and brings in the death of Christ as an illustration. He assumes that his readers already have some knowledge of the victory of Christ over evil powers, and how it was achieved. But what comes out in the passage is that Christ, no doubt by bearing our penalty, completely cancelled everything that held us under condemnation of the law. Moreover, he shifted the attention of the powers of darkness from us to himself, and forced them to make a stand against him. In such a conflict he outwitted and shamed them. As the NEB puts it, 'He discarded the cosmic powers and authorities like a garment; he made a public spectacle of them and led them as captives in his triumphal procession.'

In being defeated, Christ's enemies were totally exposed. Paul stresses this point. Neither exposure without defeat nor defeat without exposure would have dealt sufficiently with evil. Jesus, in his confrontation with the authorities who crucified him, roused them into a full-scale attack on himself, and yet made such a deceptive, disarming show of weakness that they suspected no danger and kept no reserves. To some extent they were cheated in being defeated. Paul brings out this point in his first letter to the Corinthians. The crucifixion of Jesus, he asserts, was an extremely stupid act of self-destruction on the part of this world's rulers. If they had had any wisdom they would not have crucified the Lord of glory. But they were led to their act of extreme folly by the vastly superior 'wisdom of God', and they were completely overcome by a force they had thought foolish and weak (2:8; 1:20, 27).

The fact that the cross decisively settled the conflict between God and evil is brought out again in Revelation 12. Here the writer seems to be looking at what took place in heaven while Christ was being crucified on earth. In v. 7 we read that there was 'war in heaven'. In this war Michael and his archangels overcame the dragon, destroyed completely his heavenly power, and cast him down to earth where for a short time he enjoys a restricted though enraged activity before he is to be finally destroyed. This seems to fit exactly into what Jesus accomplished in the hour of his death, and the doxology in the passage indicates that the work of defeating and casting down the dragon was really effected by Christ himself, who, we will remember, saw the beginning of his own work as the beginning of the fall of Satan from on high. The passage from the Apocalypse points out that although on earth we have to endure the vigorous activity of the defeated powers of evil until the last day, nevertheless as our 'accuser' before God the devil has no power left (Luke 10:18; Rev. 12:10). This seems to offer assurance that, however much we may be hampered by the power of evil on the earth, we will always have complete liberty and joy – especially from the accusations of the law – in our communion with God.

THE ATONEMENT AS A FOCAL POINT OF REVELATION

Our discussion of the cross as a revelation of God's love has come almost at the end of our discussion of its other central aspects. For it is through his work that God chiefly reveals himself, and we must first try to understand and appreciate his work – its purpose, its cost, its lavishness, its beauty, its effectiveness – so that we can interpret it as a revelation of God himself.

Jesus was aware that people would understand fully his life and ministry only when they saw him, as it were, 'lifted up' on the cross (John 3:14), just as Moses in the camp of Israel lifted up to view the brazen serpent as an antidote for the plague of serpents. In the course of his ministry his own brothers did not believe in him, and could not see in him what he claimed was there. They pressed him to go up to Jerusalem and make it clear who he really was and what he had come to do. 'Show yourself to the world,' was their challenge. Jesus could only reply (and they must have thought it lame), 'My time has not yet come.' He could only appear to the world as one who went about saying 'Your sins are forgiven' (John 7:4–5; Mark 2:5). Only on Calvary would people begin to see what that word really meant and cost.

Later, however, when Philip challenged him to make what he was talking about clear and easy to see, he no longer put him off as he had his brothers. For his hour of revelation was come. 'He who has seen me, has seen the Father,' he said. It was a reproach and a fresh challenge to Philip to pray for the eyes to see what he should have already seen. But it was also a challenge at this late hour to keep awake, and look more intently than ever before at his master. He was to see Jesus go to Gethsemane to pray to the Father for mercy for himself and others, he was to see Jesus die, committing himself into his Father's hands; and he was to look behind and beyond the weakness, the horror, the darkness, the treachery, the cynicism, the utter defeat, the delay, the silence, the empty tomb (John 14:8–9).

The completed work on the cross teaches us that the death of Christ is supremely the revelation of God's love. Paul might have been thinking of the actual geometrical extension of the cross when he wrote his prayer to the Ephesians that they might come to comprehend the 'breadth and length and height and depth, and to know the love of Christ which surpasses knowledge'. 'God shows his love' here, as if in the only way he can, especially in a hostile world where it shines out all the more wonderfully because no one around either wants it or deserves it, indeed, because all are enemies (Eph. 3:18–19; Rom. 5:8).

It is to the Gospel of John that we owe the text 'God so loved the world . . .' and it is in his Epistle that we see most clearly what Leon Morris calls the 'revelatory function' of the cross[15] –

By this we know love, that he laid down his life for us.

In this the love of God was made manifest among us, that God sent his only Son into the world, so that we might live through him. In this is love, not that we loved God but that he loved us and sent his Son to be the expiation for our sins.

We have an advocate with the Father, Jesus Christ the righteous; and he is the expiation for our sins, and not for ours only but also for the sins of the whole world (1 John 3:16, RSV; 4:10; 2:1–2, AV).

We do not even begin to know what love is until we understand what love is *here*. What we call love must be evaluated and brought into conformity with this love through its inspiration alone. And if our so-called 'love' is judged and condemned by what we find here, it should be called by a more appropriate name – 'lust' or 'self-seeking' would often fit better.

In the last citation love is universal. We have found no ground so far in the New Testament for suggesting that God limited the scope of his love or that Christ died only for the elect. The phrase Jesus used in calling his death a 'ransom *for many*' gives us no basis for a theory of 'limited' atonement. The phrase comes from a poem in the Old Testament which contains no thought of an arithmetic or logic of the atonement. Moreover Jesus' prayer in John 17, in which he prays not for the world but for the elect, gains its fervour from the sorrowing of one who has come to die for all, and yet has been rejected. Everything we have said in spontaneous gratitude about the cross would have to be toned down beyond recognition if it were not for all. And how could any of us ever be sure that 'his death was for me' if it were not also for all? Could John have possibly inserted 'the whole world' if this was not what he meant?

In the RSV translation, which we are using in this book, the word 'expiation' replaces the AV 'propitiation'. Looking at the texts before us, we now see some justice in Leon Morris's protest against the change of word. 'That which shows us the love of God is that which is concerned with the removal of wrath, for the act of propitiation is performed by none less than God himself in the person of his Son.'[16]

THE ATONEMENT AS EFFECTING SALVATION

Salvation – future hope and present reality

The word salvation comes from the Old Testament. It was used, along with 'redemption', to describe what God accomplished for his people in bringing them out of Egypt. Later a similar 'salvation' or 'redemption' was accomplished in their deliverance from Babylon. The great prophets, remembering such events, looked forward to a final salvation when he would bring his people fully into the Messianic age.[17]

When Paul wanted a word which would embrace every aspect of what Christ has done, and can do, for us and in us, he used the word salvation. It is true that Jesus himself referred to the consummation of his work as a 'regeneration' or 'all things made new', and he saw this taking place when he came again in his glory (cf. Matt. 19:28). But this is exactly what Paul meant when he spoke of our salvation. It will be seen and experienced in its fullness only when, having been justified and sanctified in Christ, we shall finally be 'glorified' with him. Meanwhile we are to wait in hope for our salvation and to move as far and as quickly as we can towards it (Rom. 8:30; 1 Thess. 5:8; Rom. 5:10).

But something of the glory and newness of the age to come has already been given to us here and now. Several times Paul refers to the Holy Spirit as already experienced by us as a 'pledge' or 'down-payment' of our future inheritance. This implies, as V. P. Furnish points out, that 'in the present dwelling of the Spirit in believers themselves, the power of the coming age . . . has already broken in.'[18] The age to come actually overlaps the present. Paul can indeed speak of the gift of the Spirit as being to us the 'first fruits of the harvest to come' (Rom. 8:23, NEB; cf. Heb. 6:4).

Paul was overjoyed when he saw miraculous signs taking place in his churches and when he was able to preach with manifestly powerful results. His joy was due to the fact that for him the Holy Spirit who produced such signs was 'the Spirit of promise' (Eph. 1:13). This does not mean simply a promised entity (it is a pity that both the NEB and the Jerusalem Bible have missed the point in the translation 'the promised Spirit'); but 'a power representative of the coming age which is already operative in the present'. 'The Spirit does not just precede the coming age but actually bears it, and represents the power of that age.'[19]

In the New Testament, salvation is spoken of as a powerful ongoing process which is already within us and around us. Christians are those who are 'being saved' (1 Cor. 1:18; 2 Cor. 2:15; 3:18; Rom. 1:16). Paul greets his readers in Ephesians 1 with such thrilling confidence and joy in the glory and wealth of our present possessions in Christ that we are left feeling that perhaps little awaits us in the future except the revelation of what we already have.[20] If Christians are being saved here and now then they must give evidence of this in their transformed lives. 'Now is the day of salvation,' said Paul to the Corinthians – with emphasis on the *now* (2 Cor. 6:2). This was not an evangelistic appeal to those outside the faith, but an exhortation to those within to show that the saving power of the new age was already altering completely their way of life.

To Paul the fact that 'we are *now* justified by Christ's blood' meant that we must *now* be saved by his life. And since there is *now* 'no condemnation to those who are in Christ Jesus' we must expect the law of the Spirit of life in Christ to free us from all bondage (Rom. 5:9, 10; 8:1–2). Yet, of course, while basically free, we are still badly hampered in the realisation of our salvation. We are still subject to sin, weakness and decay. The 'flesh' can be so strong even in a Christian as to thwart the impulses of the Spirit and bring defeat where there has been victory. The children of God must continue to wait, sigh and groan.[21] This side of the Christian life is fully covered in most theological writing today, and we need not say too much about it.

The death of Christ and present salvation

Certain great events are clearly crucial in world history. From the day they happened areas of community life and history began to be re-oriented in a new, and often better, direction. They injected something immediate into the stream of time that influenced, and so lives on in, the course of subsequent events. Yet their impression is less marked with time: essentially they lie in the past.

For Paul the cross and resurrection of Jesus were much more than crucial events belonging to the past. Rather they were events to be proclaimed and *re*-presented to the minds of men and women freshly and powerfully, time and again, day after day, week after week, generation after generation – as long as history lasted. In this way men and women can continually re-experience their first witness and sustain unaltered the same faith, repentance and assurance; both the church and the world can gain fresh momentum as the completion of salvation draws nearer. The miracle of their re-presentation to every age as powerful, once-for-all events takes place through the preaching of the Word and the celebration of the sacraments. Paul believed that as long as history lasted and the cross of Christ was preached it would always re-present the 'power of God' 'unto salvation' (1 Cor. 1:23–4; Rom. 1:16).

We can understand why Paul insisted that the churches of his day must always experience in their personal and community life the transforming, spiritual power of salvation. Otherwise – without such signs of salvation – were they not declaring to the world that the cross had lost its transforming power and that Christ had died in vain?

The death of Christ and human history

A vivid picture is given to us in Revelation 5. It shows more clearly than elsewhere in the New Testament the general relation between the death of Jesus and the great on-going work of salvation which is to find its climax in the second coming of Christ.

John, admitted to heaven, sees the throne of God. He takes his place in the congregation and sees at the right hand of God a book with seven seals; but it is closed and no one is found worthy to break its seals. John weeps bitterly, for it is the breaking of seal after seal that is to set in motion the history of salvation on earth, and to lead to the final coming of the kingdom there. Until the book is opened, earth's history will be left to course aimlessly. But suddenly there appears in heaven 'a lamb standing as though it had been slain, with seven horns and seven eyes, which are the seven spirits of God sent into all the earth'. A doxology is sung. Seal after seal is opened, and history is set in its true motion: the kingdom comes.

History is ruled, and the destiny of mankind is controlled, by the lamb. It is the cross that gives him the right to exercise his rule – 'Worthy art thou to take the scroll and to open its seals, for thou wast slain . . .' Moreover, because he was slain he has the power of the seven spirits of God which go into 'all the earth' to make manifest and relevant throughout history what he has done for mankind in his death and resurrection. ('Dear dying Lamb, thy precious blood shall never lose its power' – Cowper.) Thus the cross continually injects into the course of human affairs the momentum that will inevitably carry history on to its destiny.[22]

The cross, salvation and the wrath of God

It is when discussing salvation or redemption that Paul mentions most the wrath of God, and our being delivered from it.

In the Old Testament the fact that God has anger is reflected in what he does (see pp. 5–7). The effects of his wrath are often seen in catastrophes, devastating defeats, or plagues which visit those who deliberately thwart his will, and in the prevalence of corruption, decay and death (cf. Ps. 90). But these phenomena are only signs – very *restrained* signs – that God has anger. Nothing of earth or humankind could remain if God vented his anger.

But *whenever* we see signs on earth that remind us of our frailty, of our deeply tragic existence, we are meant to realise that behind the manifestation of God's judgment there is God's own inward reaction and hatred of our sin that we cannot begin to conceive. It is only because he restrains this, within himself, that we are not consumed (Lam. 3:22). We noted in our Old Testament study how God appears to struggle with himself to control himself. God's wrath is always exercised alongside his grace and mercy. In the Bible, as Markus Barth points out, the 'wrath' of God '. . . does not represent the intemperate outburst of an uncontrolled character. It is rather the temperature of God's love, the manifestation of the will and power to resist, to overcome, to turn away all that contradicts the counsels of his love.'[23]

In the New Testament we read no more of God's struggle with anger. The emphasis is on his grace. We are meant to understand that he has dealt with his wrath fully and finally in Jesus Christ. He has passed his righteous judgment against sin, and put wrath away. We must think about this when we think of what Jesus went through in his dereliction on the cross. We are not told directly that Christ bore the 'wrath of God'. But Paul dares to say that Christ bore our curse – and as Markus Barth again observes, 'curse is infinitely worse than wrath.'[24] Yet the New Testament, while it ceases to speak further of God's feelings of wrath, often speaks of the tempered, restrained expressions of God's wrath that feature so prominently in the Old Testament. These continue to be a feature of the life of the world under the New Testament. In the first chapters of Romans Paul describes how God 'gives up' those who practise evil to fearful processes of moral degeneration. While they remain alive, increasing criminality and cruelty, the unnatural and perverse, a hardening heart and even self-annihilation is their lot. The strictures and even the tyrannies of civil government are sometimes the instrument of this 'wrath' (Rom. 1:18–32; cf. 1 Thess. 2:16; Eph. 5:6; Rom. 13:4 ff).

This form of 'wrath' threatens Christians too, while they live as part of a human society that is under it. But in their case God tempers the processes. Even his wrath may be expressed graciously and quietly, in a Fatherly way, so that it becomes a 'chastening' rather than a punishment (Heb. 12:6; Rom. 3:19; 2 Cor. 6:9). In this way they are 'saved from wrath', and since there is no restraint on God's love towards them there need never be any restraint in the boldness of their approach to him.

In the last days, however, the restraints at present exercised over the expressions of evil and the 'wrath of God' will be removed – we have a picture in the book of Revelation of the seven cups full of the 'wrath of God' being poured out on the nations who reject God's salvation and mercy. Yet at this second point of desperate need, those who trust in the mercy of God are still 'saved from the wrath to come' (Rev. 15–16; 1 Thess. 1:10; 5:9).

4 Sanctification in the New Testament

THE CONSTRAINT OF THE CROSS TO NEWNESS OF LIFE

Sanctification means the hallowing of a place or object, or human life, so that it can be rescued from the service of evil and set apart to the service and use of God. For individuals it is almost the same as repentance – our turning or conversion from our old evil ways to a new life.

According to Paul the love of Christ 'controls' us[1] and the righteousness of God revealed in the cross has assumed a pressing nature. The cross of Christ has intensified the sin of the world. Before Jesus came there was a distance between man and God. God was reserved in his condemnation of our sin, and man could avoid a full and final confrontation with God. But, in Jesus, God himself came, as it were, to live in the same house with us. It is a house not big enough for two unless one yields to the rights of the other. God has allowed his affairs and claims to become so mixed up with ours that the decisions of each about the other are bound to come to a head.

Jesus felt this constraint, and he spoke of the overwhelming pressure or 'distress' moving him towards the cross (Luke 12:50). He warned that the cross would bring the 'world' into profound tension, and it would find itself called to repentance. 'Now is the judgment of this world' (John 12:31). Things that were true, right and of real worth would be crucified in him because in their true form the world hated them. Only one hope remained for a world such as this. It must reassess what it had done, acknowledge the falseness and stupidity of its standard of values, and the perversity of its way. It must accept the judgment passed on it, and take the way to new life. It must 'begin to love the things that it had hated and to hate the things that it loved'.[2]

In Isaiah 53, a passage so prominent in the mind of Jesus, we find that many in the community which killed the servant of God experienced this kind of radical repentance. After the servant died they looked back on what he had been, and on what they had rejected in rejecting him. They found themselves judged because of their former false values and choices. 'He was despised' – twice they repeated it to their own shame, for this was their sin. And this was their confession to each other: 'we esteemed him not.' No doubt their desire to change everything from then on was expressed in their resolve that the servant would yet 'see the fruit of the travail of his soul and be satisfied' (Isa. 53:3, 11).

At the time of Pentecost the thoughts of the apostle Peter revolved around this chapter of Isaiah. His speeches, preaching and prayers recorded in the earliest chapters of Acts show its influence. Jesus was the 'servant' (Acts 3:13, 26; 4:27, 30), and in crucifying him the world had proved that the only place it had reserved for God's goodness was indeed on a cross! They had preferred Barabbas to Jesus, rejecting God's 'righteous servant'. 'You denied the holy and righteous one,' Peter said, 'and asked for a murderer to be granted to you, and killed the Author of life, whom God raised from the dead' (Acts 3:14–15). It was powerful preaching, and Peter's closing call to a people 'cut to its heart' was, 'Repent and be baptised every one of you in the name of Jesus Christ.' It was a call for a complete change of thought as well as of ways – for a revaluation of all their values in the light of the judgment clearly pronounced upon them in the cross.[3]

In a later letter to Christians in Asia Minor, Peter's tone is gentler, but he presents the appeal of the cross for a change of attitude and life in an even more compelling way. We have to yield to Jesus because:

He himself bore our sins in his body on the tree, that we might die to sin and live to righteousness. By his wounds you have been healed. For you were straying like sheep, but have now returned to the Shepherd and Guardian of your souls.

Christ also died for sins once for all, the righteous for the unrighteous that he might bring us to God (1 Pet. 2:24–5; 3:18).

They were reminded of the change Christ had already made in their lives through his sacrifice. As 'wandering sheep', they had been lost in the great, bewildering and cruel gentile world. They had not known how to find order and meaning in life. But Jesus had taken them over as their 'shepherd' and 'guardian' and had given them a worthwhile purpose, a direction, and an assurance that now their effort was not in vain.

But if ever they were tempted to forget or grow careless, they were reminded of what the change cost the Redeemer: 'By his wounds you have been healed.' In giving them healing Jesus had taken from them – his wounds! They had certainly not been there physically to wound him, but Peter knew that they *felt* they had been there, and that they, too, had contributed to what had bowed his head. Like those described in Isaiah 53, they had felt that their own indifference, carelessness and hostility were responsible for the wounding of Jesus.[4] They were to remember, too, that the sins of which his wounds reminded them were actually the burden that made Jesus give way in his agony of dereliction and death – only to be upheld by God alone: 'He himself bore our sins in his body.' At the same time Peter encouraged them with a further thought: that Christ not only 'bore our sins on the tree' but, as it were, handed them over to God for disposal. The NEB puts it well: 'In his own person he carried our sins up to the gibbet.'

The older translations of the Bible sometimes encourage us with the thought that in Christ our sins are 'covered' (cf. Ps. 32:1). But today the idea of a 'cover-up' has bad associations. Indeed, the problem of our past often appears to us like the problem of used nuclear material which cannot simply be 'covered'. What about the waste product of our sin? We may be pronounced 'forgiven', but do not the effects of past evils sink into our subconscious minds and there distort the way we think and live from day to day? And do they not spread abroad entirely beyond our control, affecting the lives of other people? And will they not have their effects on future generations?

The newer translations of the Bible tend to talk of our sins being 'done away', rather than 'covered', and Peter does seem to be trying to convey this idea when he speaks of Christ taking our sins 'up to the gibbet'. The implication is that a safe place of disposal is found with God for this polluting waste product. It is dealt with and its ultimate consequences are nullified. In the later passage in the epistle Peter tries to reinforce this message with the assurance that Christ died to sin 'once for all' – no repetition of this sacrifice will ever be needed, nor will anything ever be required to supplement it.

All these thoughts about the cross are in Peter's exposition a reminder to his readers that they not only are called to newness of life but that they have the freedom to hear and to respond to the constraining word of the cross.

FOLLOWING THE CRUCIFIED ONE ON THE WAY TO GOD

In the same context in which he speaks of Christ as bearing our sins up to the tree, Peter refers to Christ's refusal to revile when he was reviled, or to threaten when he suffered, and to his obedient commitment of himself to God. In all this he 'suffered for you, leaving you an example that you should follow in his steps' (1 Pet. 2:20–3).

Peter has no hesitation in emphasising certain features of Jesus' attitude and conduct as he faced the cross, for their indirect imitation by his readers. They too had their particular cross to face. For slaves and underlings in that world this meant buckling down under a corrupt bureaucracy, being deprived of their basic human rights (those they knew Jesus had come to secure for all mankind), accepting the strictures of foolish laws and ruthless, immoral masters (often pharisaical hypocrites). They were to remember and follow exactly the pattern of the life of the crucified one who had come in this precise way to 'lead them to God' (1 Pet. 3:18).

Peter's suggestion that we should imitate the crucified one offers us scope for a much fuller expression of all that Jesus taught, and died for, than is at first obvious from Peter's narrow application of the principle to the concrete situation before his readers. On the way to the cross Jesus was radiantly thankful. The Lord's Supper was a 'eucharist' or 'thanksgiving', and in celebrating it he was joyful and peaceful (John 15:11; 14:27). On his way to the cross his attitude to the civil authorities was marked as much by an intransigent inner resistance to everything they stood for, as by a humble submission to their courts and judgment. They were on trial much more than he. He dictated the pace of the events, laying down his life rather than having it taken away. He expressed deep concern for the 'city', its twisted politics and social injustices. He did not neglect the needs of his own mother, and had time to save a soul while he founded a church (John 10:18; Luke 13:34; 19:41; John 19:26; Luke 23:42–3).

It is true that Jesus did not teach much directly about our modern problems of an advanced technology, medical ethics, over-population or ecology. But in the pattern of his own life and attitude we have quite basic guidelines, and we have his promise that light will be given to us on many problems as we 'seek first' the kingdom of God (Matt. 6:33). We can affirm that at least we have a very important core-pattern which must have a profound effect on our ethical thinking. We are certainly not left to 'love God and do what you like' under the supposed influence of a 'Spirit' unpatterned and unethical in its expressions.

No doubt Peter derived his principle of imitating Jesus on his way to the cross from our Lord's own teaching: 'If any man would come after me, let him deny himself and take up his cross and follow me. For whoever would save his life will lose it, and whoever loses his life for my sake will find it. For what will it profit a man, if he gains the whole world and forfeits his life?' (Matt. 16:24–6). At the time it was spoken, this saying referred to the hard, taxing demands that were to be made on Jesus' contemporary band of disciples as they stayed with him on his way to his death. But it applies no less to what faces every generation of Christians as they answer his call to discipleship. Jesus affirmed that each one of his disciples will hear his 'voice' and know him or herself led through life in obedience to it, and in his presence (John 10:1 ff). It is possible for the Christian to be led only if there is a constant, stern denial of all self-will, and indeed of all desire for self-development. This will be the first crucial test of ability to follow. The second test will be that of accepting and bearing with willing alacrity whatever load of suffering or persecution may be incurred if the appointed way is to be travelled. And all this is to be done in imitation of his own saving work, in the belief that it is he who is calling for it to be done for his sake and in his service.

What matters most is facing the cross with the same submissive attitude and the same rebellious and victorious action which characterised Jesus in his passion, and which he expected to be duplicated within the life of the Christian. If this is faced then all other things will indeed take their proper place, and other ethical problems will be met as they arise.[5]

Peter's suggestion that Jesus on his way to the cross set a core-pattern for our Christian behaviour is further illustrated and reinforced by Paul's discussion of the saving obedience of Christ:

Then as one man's tresspass led to condemnation for all men, so one man's act of righteousness leads to acquittal and life for all men. For as by one man's disobedience many were made sinners, so by one man's obedience many will be made righteous (Rom. 5:18–19).

The life of Jesus from his birth to his death is regarded as having redemptive value, and is oriented towards its climax in his death. He saved us by a lifelong obedience as well as by offering his life in death as a sacrifice. Moreover, the 'obedience' which Paul here stresses is Jesus' obedience not simply as the Messiah of Israel but rather as the second Adam. He saves us by reversing the curse and death which came upon mankind through the disobedience of Adam. As we all fell and died in Adam, so we all live and rise in Christ. As we are all condemned through Adam's sin, so we all have acquittal through Christ's 'act of righteousness' (1 Cor. 15:21–2; Rom. 5:18).

In thinking of Christ's 'obedience' as pleasing God and cancelling out the curse that fell on mankind, it is helpful to use the distinction later drawn by theologians between Christ's 'passive' and 'active' obedience. His passive obedience consisted of his acceptance of the curse of the law, the penalty of sin, the judgment of God, and all the other acquiescent aspects of his suffering. His active obedience consisted of the way in which, throughout the whole course of his life, he perfectly observed the law and lived in true righteousness and love. His was a sinless life of trust in his Father. Paul implies here that God approved and accepted as redemptive Christ's passive obedience in suffering and also his active obedience in daily living. He not only voiced his approval from heaven at the baptism and the transfiguration, not only gave signs of approval in the miracles Jesus accomplished, but finally raised him from the dead and took him up to heaven in the humanity in which this obedience had been offered. Such a final significant seal of approval is equivalent to God's saying: This is the kind of human response to my love that perfectly pleases me – and this is the pattern of what I will to accept and have before me for ever.

THE WORK OF THE SPIRIT IN THE SANCTIFICATION OF CHRIST AND THE CHRISTIAN

The New Testament speaks of Christ as not only obedient to God, but also as 'sanctifying' himself or as being 'sanctified' in offering his life and death to God. He had one aim – to please his Father. He did not seek selfish gain or human approval or angelic applause. He set his eyes singly on God. His sanctification is simply his obedience viewed in this light (cf. John 8:29; 10:36; 17:19; Matt. 6:22; Heb. 2:1).

An important passage in the Epistle to the Hebrews stresses the work of the Spirit in the sanctification of Christ. The writer of this Epistle interprets the work of Jesus as the fulfilment of the Old Testament sacrifices (8:1). He begins by showing that Christ was honoured by God because on earth he was contented to accept the form of an obedient, praying, suffering servant of God, a man of humble sympathy. He has therefore been exalted to a unique, eternal high priesthood. The writer goes on to compare the offerings of the Jewish priests in the old sanctuary to what Christ offers in his heavenly sanctuary. The priest's offerings had only an anticipatory and partial efficacy, but Christ by one offering has once for all fully accomplished everything that other offerings aimed at with only temporary effect:

He entered once for all into the Holy Place, taking not the blood of goats and calves, but his own blood, thus securing an eternal redemption. For if the sprinkling of defiled persons with the blood of goats and bulls and with the ashes of a heifer sanctifies for the purification of the flesh, how much more shall the blood of Christ, who through the eternal Spirit offered himself without blemish to

God, purify your conscience from dead works to serve the living God (Heb. 9:12–15).

The thought is clear. The 'blood' of Christ, the saving efficacy of which is the theme of so many hymns, is Christ himself. He shed his blood by pouring himself out in a life of obedience. It was with this self-effusion that he entered the sanctuary with redeeming power, and made his perfect offering to God.

It was 'through the eternal Spirit' that Christ was sanctified and enabled to offer himself 'without spot' to God. From the moment of his birth the grace of God was with him, forming his life through the power of the Spirit into one of perfect obedience to God. His human goodness, beauty and love were the work of the Spirit, as was his power to offer himself trustfully to God in the critical moments of his final agony.

The same eternal Spirit can and will sanctify us to follow him, and will duplicate within our lives today what he did for the Saviour. Indeed we can be suspicious of any supposed work of the Spirit that does not produce within us, even if only faintly, what was produced first in Jesus.

The writer of the Epistle was convinced that the 'Word of God' can penetrate deep into the subconscious levels of the human mind. He describes it as 'living and active, sharper than any two-edged sword, piercing to the division of soul and spirit, of joints and marrow, and discerning the thoughts and intentions of the heart' (4:12). In our present text the 'Spirit' of God and the 'blood of Christ' are regarded as having their effect at exactly the same deepest level of human existence. That the blood of Christ will 'purge our conscience' means that it will work as the Spirit works with transforming power at exactly those levels at which today psychoanalysis tries to penetrate, in order to cure us of the neuroses which so often spoil our living.

The cure this deep surgery will effect in our daily life will show itself in a new integrity between heart and action. To be 'delivered from dead works to serve the living God' will mean always coming into touch with the reality and presence of God when we hear the Word of God, or celebrate the sacrament of the Lord's Supper, or pray. It will mean an end to listlessness and dead formality in our worship and other service of God. It will mean doing what we do for Christ's sake with all our heart and soul and strength and mind (Luke 10:27).

THE SANCTIFICATION OF THE CHRISTIAN IN CHRIST

The Epistle to the Hebrews, when discussing our sanctification, often omits mention of the Spirit; the work of our sanctification is regarded as directly that of Christ himself (Heb. 2:11). Jesus, it is stated, was 'sanctified' i.e., made fit or 'perfect' for his work by God, especially by means of the sufferings he had to undergo.[6] But later in the Epistle it is brought out that in and through this sanctification of Jesus we too are already made perfect and sanctified. Indeed we are 'sanctified' once for all through the offering of the body of Jesus Christ (10:14, 29).

In the Gospel of John we find the same thought. We are sanctified or 'consecrated' to the service of God in and through Jesus himself. He describes himself as the one whom the Father consecrated and sent into the world, and he consecrates himself so that the disciples whom he is sending out might be 'consecrated by the truth' (John 10:36; 17:17–19).

Paul's letters take us even further into the mystery of our sanctification being already completed in Christ. Paul's references to Jesus as the second Adam or the 'man from heaven' show that he regarded Christ's human nature as representative of the whole people of God, and indeed of the whole human race. In this Paul was no doubt following up Jesus' own reference to himself as the Son of man (cf. p. 27). Since Jesus himself included us in what he was doing, Paul sees not only our reconciliation and justification as being completed in Christ, but also our sanctification. With this in mind he speaks of Christ as being the one 'whom God made our wisdom, our righteousness and sanctification and redemption'. 'You who were once estranged,' he writes to the Colossians, 'he has now reconciled in his body of flesh by his death in order to present you holy and blameless and irreproachable before him' (1 Cor. 1:30; Col. 1:21–2).

Paul obviously expected his congregations to make every effort to progress in working out their sanctification for themselves by the grace of Christ. But essential to their success was their realisation that Christ had already worked it out for them in his own life. Thus to encourage the Corinthians, who were so far from their goal of becoming Christ-like, to persevere towards it, he reminded them that Jesus had already achieved it for them. 'You were washed, you were sanctified, you were justified in the name of the Lord Jesus Christ and in the Spirit of our God' (1 Cor. 6:11).

The way Paul speaks of this mystery implies that it is not merely a pattern of our sanctification, but an accomplished reality – our actual sanctification itself – that we find worked out in Christ. Calvin in his attempt to express this stressed that Christ was not simply the 'instrument' but the 'matter' of our salvation. This means that when we seek our sanctification we do not need to strive to work it out from scratch within ourselves. Rather we 'put on' what is already there in Christ to be given to us as his gift; and we receive our sanctification as we receive him, coming to have him 'in us', and coming to be ourselves 'in Him'.[7]

What has been said in this section, and what has already been said about the work of the Spirit in our sanctification, underline that the Spirit brings into our lives only what was first produced in Jesus Christ himself and reproduces within us nothing that was not first in him.[8]

THE PARTICIPATION OF THE CHRISTIAN IN THE DYING OF CHRIST

Paul dwells often on the thought of our participation in, or our fellowship with, the dying and rising of Christ. He can speak of himself not only as being united to Christ but as being 'crucified with Christ', and of our having died and risen with Christ.[9] This thought is further developed in his Epistle to the Philippians, where he expresses his desire to know Christ 'and the power of his resurrection, and may share his sufferings, becoming like him in his death, that if possible I may attain to the resurrection from the dead' (3:10–11). He believes that the future pattern of his life, in which his salvation will be worked out, will repeat the pattern set in the death and resurrection of Christ, and that he will achieve salvation by the power he receives through sharing in the dying and rising of Jesus himself.

Elsewhere Paul speaks of himself as 'always carrying in the body the death of Jesus, so that the life of Jesus may also be manifested in our bodies' (2 Cor. 4:10). He implies that there is a power in Christ's saving activity which is communicated to the church and to Christians to enable us to conform to him. He discusses this subject in a most difficult and controversial passage in the Epistle to the Colossians (1:24). He is speaking of how he rejoices in his suffering for the sake of his readers, and he adds, 'and in my flesh I complete what is lacking in Christ's afflictions for the sake of his body, that is, the church'.

Though some aspect of what Paul calls 'Christ's afflictions for the sake of his body' has yet in some way to be undergone to make up its full account, we need not therefore conclude that Paul regards the sufferings of Christ on the cross as themselves insufficient or incomplete. Paul would without doubt have agreed with the affirmation of the Epistle to the Hebrews, 'By a single offering he has perfected for all time those who are sanctified' (10:14).

It has been suggested that Paul intended simply to accuse the Colossians of not yielding themselves to participate fully in Christ's sufferings, thus involving Paul with the undue responsibility of extra care for them. D. Whiteley, along a similar vein, suggests that one of the lasting effects of Christ's once-for-all death was a 'reflection in the church of his suffering'. Just as the moon reflects without supplementing the light of the sun, so the church reflects in its life without supplementing the sufferings of Christ.[10]

However T. W. Manson seems to give the most satisfactory view of this passage. He links up Paul's thought here with Jesus' own words about his baptism and cup, and with the Old Testament idea of the remnant as it was fulfilled in the life of Jesus. For Jesus, the road to the cross is a road of ever-increasing loneliness, and at the end of it Jesus is absolutely alone. From that point onwards, if we read Paul aright, there is an ever-increasing fellowship of the sufferings of Christ. The prophecy of Jesus is fulfilled: 'The cup that I drink ye shall drink: and with the baptism that I am baptised withal shall ye be baptised.' This word could not be fulfilled in his lifetime; it is fulfilled after and through his death and resurrection.[11]

Whatever view we take when interpreting these passages, they reiterate the call to have always before us the image of the one who died and rose again, and to leave our lives open to the inner power that is especially promised to us as we seek to conform to him.

THE SANCTIFICATION OF DEATH IN THE DEATH OF CHRIST

Paul speaks of death as a natural enemy to human life and well-being. God's original purpose for mankind may have included some kind of transition from the present world to another life, but such a transition was never meant to be accomplished by our being subjected to such corruption and dissolution as we see taking place when death strikes human life. For Paul death has a 'sting' from which we need to be delivered.

Christ has altered death itself; he has removed its sting so that in effect death has been 'abolished'. Our experience of dying on earth can itself become an important part of our sanctification, forming the completion of our own 'dying with Christ', and, as Luther pointed out, of our baptism into Christ. Paul could look on the passage through death as the glorious completion of his life (1 Cor. 15:26; 2 Tim. 1:10;

Phil. 1:21). Yet for Christ to die demanded costly effort at a costly price. He 'tasted death for every man', says the writer to the Hebrews. He feared his death and cried to God to be delivered from it. We are meant, when we read these descriptions, to think of the 'cup' from which he shrank in Gethsemane. Speaking of Jesus' resurrection, Peter affirmed that it took place because God 'loosed' for him 'the pangs of death' (Heb. 2:9; 5:7; Acts 2:24).

Apart from the fellowship of Christ in and through death, it still remains dreadful, especially because it brings people nearer to the exposure and judgment of our lives by God, when the 'books' are opened and we stand before him. Here again, the one who died is the advocate, friend and justifier of his people in face of such an ordeal (Rev. 20:11–12; 1 John 2:1).

PART 2

THE ATONEMENT IN THE HISTORY OF CHRISTIAN THOUGHT

5 The formulation of doctrine

THE FACT AND THE THEORY

> Christ died for our sins in accordance with the scriptures . . . he was buried . . . he was raised on the third day in accordance with the scriptures (1 Cor. 15:3–4).

We have indicated our belief that the death of Christ was central to the thinking of the New Testament writers about God, man, and life itself. It was the cross that they spoke about first of all in their summary of the Gospel. It was towards the cross that they turned to experience the power of God, the forgiveness of sins and newness of life and to know and see the face of God and his glory. They expected their congregations to have 'fellowship' with them in the same liberating, joyful experience of forgiveness of sins and eternal life (1 John 1:3; John 1:3; 2:1). Jesus, they knew, had prayed for 'those who are to believe in me' through the word they had been given to share with all around them, 'that they too might behold my glory' (John 17:20, 24).

We do not have to look far to find ample evidence of the fulfilment of such a promise. It is apparent when we read how the death of Christ was understood and preached by the Fathers and theologians of the later church. It is worth quoting the testimony of one who was, comparatively speaking, almost as distant from the original event as we are, and who found its meaning and centrality as seriously questioned as it is today.

> The death of the Saviour [wrote Dora Greenwell in a letter to Professor Knight of St Andrews on June 6, 1868] remains for me just what it is, a fact – Heaven's unexplained enigma – but the one which alone to my heart meets and touches all life's direst needs. It is more real than anything in the world, or out of it; that which

brings the pitying, sympathising element into the whirl and awful chaos of creation; it makes of God a Being to be loved, because it proves that there is a necessity (of nature unknown to us) for the loss, anguish, and death that possess the whole world, *and that God himself has stooped to it*. How different from the old gods of Greece, careless and cruel in their continual serenity – a *God upon a cross*. This, as Lacordaire says, is my theology: *Summa Theologiae*. The aspect in which I see the cross (since I saw it at all) never varies. It has saved the world, and it will save me.[1]

When we give our complete attention to the voice of the New Testament writers, and when we look at what they are pointing to, their witness conveys the convincing assurance that the power and guilt of our past human sin has been annulled; that the future need raise no more fear in our minds; that whatever the depth of human suffering, God will remain with us; that whatever the chaos in our personal, family or social life, he can ultimately restore true order. 'We know that it covers everything and guarantees everything in which we are vitally interested,' says Denney, 'that it disposes of the past, creates the future, is a security for immortal life and glory.'[2] Our whole venture in seeking to understand the theology of the cross will be a mere empty academic exercise if we fail now to grasp this immediate significance of the New Testament message.

Theologians of the last century referred to the event of the cross, thus illumined for us by the New Testament witness, as the 'fact' of the cross. They regarded all further theological reflection as entering the 'theory' of the cross.[3] But for them the question became acute: if we receive so much by simply repeatedly listening to the New Testament witness, is further theory really necessary? In their day the meaning of the cross had been explained in a 'scheme of salvation' – a plan worked out in eternity by God and Christ, so simple that it could easily be understood by the ordinary human intelligence. When the time came to put the scheme into operation it was carried out to the strictest detail.

Coleridge, voicing the feelings of many, expressed contempt for this illegitimate speculation beyond what is enunciated for us in the New Testament. While we can expand on the consequences of the Redeemer's act, he insisted, we must not try to probe its cause: 'The Mysterious Act, the Operative Cause is *transcendent* – FACTUM EST.'[4]

It is true that the cross is a transcendent and mysterious act. How can we expect to understand 'clearly' when we see 'the strange sight of omnipotence embracing ignominy, of blessedness submitting itself to pain, of glory condescending to shame, of purity taking the place of sin'?[5] 'The longer the line of reflection we cast into these waters,' says A. B. Macaulay, 'the more unfathomable will their depths be found.'[6]

The darkness that descended on the earth when Christ died has often justly been taken as a symbol that here much must remain enigmatic to the human mind until the day when every shadow now over our human life has taken flight. But though surrounded and penetrated by mystery, the cross nevertheless demands from us intelligent response as well as emotional reaction. 'This cannot be grasped by loving well,' said Luther, 'it can be grasped by reason illumined by faith.'[7]

God acts often with great severity, mysteriously, in ways beyond our understanding, and 'higher than our ways' (Isa. 55:8–9). But it is a striking feature of the biblical description of God that he is never pictured as acting irrationally. And always he wants his people to understand, or to try to understand. He sends the prophets to try to help them to do so. The Fatherhood ascribed to God means that he wants to share the significance of what he does in life with his children. This is why we believe there is a meaning in the cross to be read and understood by the human mind. Paul speaks of the '*word* of the cross'. Jesus urged us to grow beyond the stage of being simply 'servants' who do not know what the master is doing, in order to become 'friends' with whom understanding is shared (1 Cor. 1:18; John 14:15).

The devout minds of the church have always felt that their faith was compelled to seek to understand what it already saw. The New Testament account of the death of Jesus forced them to ask further questions about it, and seek answers. And they had to try to hold the various statements of the New Testament together in some such way as to obtain a unified view of what was, after all, one act of the one God. They approached their task knowing that simplicity, reverence and prayer were more important than brilliance of mind. They knew themselves to be dealing with the God of Jesus Christ who had hid things from the wise and prudent and revealed them to babes (Matt. 11:25). Gradually, as time went on, they understood more, and were in a position to see still more waiting to be understood. They failed, as we shall see, only when they thought they had understood without seeing more yet to be understood.

THE DEVELOPMENT OF PARTIAL INSIGHTS

From the first century onward the church felt that it had to preserve what was distinctive in the faith. If it was to maintain its power to overcome the world, it had to keep as close as possible to the original teaching given by Jesus and by the Holy Spirit to the apostles, and handed down by genuine apostolic tradition in Holy Scripture. It became especially concerned to safeguard its teaching as to who Christ was, and how Christians might properly conceive of him. Heretical views on this subject were condemned and orthodoxy was defined in the midst of bitter conflict by a series of church councils. Those who fought for orthodoxy, often at the cost of great suffering, felt that the existence of the church was at stake unless they succeeded in rooting out false teaching.

But when it came to defining what Christ had come to *do*, especially through his death, there was no such concern, and no orthodox definition. The confession, 'Christ died for our sins according to the Scriptures,' opened up such an ample area for the imagination and thought to work on that, given an orthodox Christology, one would have to go very far indeed to go astray. In interpreting the meaning of Christ's work quite different paths could be taken. Yet all, it was felt, would lead in directions that helped the church towards fuller, clearer vision.

During the early centuries, therefore, as the church tried to express and develop the thought of the New Testament on the atonement, there arose what might be called a series of partial insights. Some Fathers stuck largely to one line of thought. They found that their chosen narrow path gave them sufficient inspiration and fullness in their apprehension of the Gospel, and they needed no other avenues to explore. Others probed everywhere. They followed predecessors only to progress beyond them, discovering new vantage points from which other followers could make their own fresh beginnings. R. S. Franks speaks, for example, of the enormous versatility of views on the work of Christ scattered throughout Augustine's writings, frequently presenting new suggestions, new combinations, new interpretations – a 'mine out of which later theologians could extract material for doctrinal development'.[8]

THE ATONEMENT AS AN INNER TRANSACTION – THE 'WONDERFUL EXCHANGE'

Augustine (354–430), illustrating in a sermon what Christ does to us in the atonement, pointed out the variety of commercial exchange: barley is exchanged for wheat, lead for silver, wool for ready-made garments – 'But no one (except Christ!) gives life to receive death!' (Sermon xxx. 5).

Several of the early Fathers saw that through the incarnation God has entered into the inner life of mankind to set up an organic union between himself and mankind. Thus an 'exchange' has been made possible and a new beginning between himself and us. The incarnation and the cross are intimately linked.

As early as the second century an unknown writer refers to the cross as such a transaction, and he uses the terminology that was often repeated by Augustine and by the Reformers two centuries afterwards:

> He himself took on him the burden of our iniquities, he gave his own Son as a ransom for us, the holy One for transgressors, the blameless One for the wicked, the righteous One for the unrighteous, the incorruptible One for the corruptible, the immortal One for them that are mortal. For what other thing was capable of covering our sins than his righteousness? By what other one was it possible that we, the wicked and ungodly, could be justified, than by the only Son of God? O benefits surpassing all expectation! that the wickedness of many should be hid in a single righteous One, and that the righteousness of One should justify many transgressors (*Epistle to Diognetus*, ch. IX).

It was *Irenaeus* (*c*. 150–200) who first (in *Against Heresies*) clearly linked this 'exchange' with the union achieved in the incarnation between the immortal Son of God and our corruptible human nature, for 'unless man had been joined to God, he could never have become a partaker of incorruptibility.' According to Irenaeus Christ saved us by reversing what had happened in Adam. Jesus 'recapitulated in himself the long line of human beings and furnished us, in a brief comprehensive manner with salvation, so that what we lost in Adam we might recover in him'. By dying he took upon himself our corruption. 'The corruptible is swallowed up by incorruptibility, the mortal by immortality, that we might receive the adoption of sons' (3:18:7; 3:19:1).

We are saved from physical corruption and death. But there are other aspects of Christ's saving work from within humanity. Irenaeus speaks of our whole human life being 'sanctified' by the obedient response of Jesus to God as he developed through the natural stages of human life (2:22:4). Moreover, Irenaeus does not believe that all men are automatically saved by the incarnation itself. He speaks of faith, and says 'knowledge' of the Son of God makes immortal those who 'receive and behold him through faith', and again, we are made immortal through seeing God and knowing him (4:20:5,6; 4:36:7). It seems that for Irenaeus the ultimate fulfilment of the 'wonderful exchange' involved, besides the incarnation, a sacramental or mystical union between Christ and the knowing, seeing believer.

Athanasius (d. 373) developed the same line of thought. He stressed the dilemma facing God in our sin. It was 'unthinkable' that God should go back on his word, and that man, having transgressed, should not die; but it was equally 'monstrous' that beings who had once shared the nature of the Word should perish. What then was God to do? In *The Incarnation of the Word*, Athanasius rejected the possibility that repentance on the part of man could cure his blindness or corruption, or lastingly guarantee his future conduct (§ 6–7). God therefore maintains the constancy of his character by 'assuming humanity' – taking a body, which is 'our body,' directly from a spotless, stainless virgin without the agency of a human father, surrendering this body, instead of all, to death, and offering it to the Father. This was done so that in his death all are held to have died, and so that the 'law with respect to the corruption of mankind' might be abolished. We now live 'through the appropriation of his body and the grace of his resurrection'. Death comes to Christ and disappears from men 'as utterly as snow from fire' (§ 8–9).

Athanasius, like Irenaeus, emphasises the solidarity of Christ and mankind that makes this exchange possible. He does not consider the atonement as having primarily a transcendent effect within God or indeed within any sphere outside the life of mankind. Death had its hold within our nature; it was 'woven into' our very substance. To deliver us from its domination life must be woven there in its place (§ 44, 47).[9] He is concerned about the spiritual – as well as the physical – effects of Christ's incarnation and death. Christ, by the grace of God, has come to make of our frail, inconsistent human nature something morally stable and sanctified.

Important in our redemption is our deliverance from error and from the worship of false gods. God has revealed his true image to us anew in Christ. He has given us this image to look at, in order to recreate us in his image. In this way he has manifested himself not only that 'we might become God' but that 'we might perceive the mind of the unseen Father' (§ 13, 54).

Athanasius writes of the inclusive and representative nature of Christ's humanity. When Jesus was anointed at his baptism, it was we who were anointed in him, and everything he received in his anointing was not for his own profit or use, but to be passed on to us (*Against the Arians*, 1:51, 47, 48).

Whereas the Greek Fathers stressed our deliverance from corruption and death, *Augustine* changes the main emphasis to our deliverance from sin and guilt. For example, in one of his sermons he engages in a favourite technique – the striking and unexpected application of the text to drive home his point and to hold his congregation. He uses Paul's word 'the Lord is at hand' to raise the question of how far apart two people can be from one another, though they are near: 'Even though they should dwell in close neighbourhood, even though they should be bound by one chain, the godly is far from the ungodly, the innocent from the guilty.' But what of God and ourselves? – for he, with 'two good things', righteousness and immortality, comes near to us who have two evil things, iniquity and mortality.

> Mark these two things. He is righteous. He is immortal. In the two evil things one is the guilt, the other is the penalty; the guilt in that thou art unrighteous, the penalty in that thou art mortal. That he might be nigh, he took thy penalty, he did not take thy guilt! . . . By taking the penalty and not taking the guilt, he effaced both the guilt and the penalty. The Lord therefore is very nigh, be careful for nothing (Serm. cxxi. 3).

THE EXTERNAL ASPECT – THE RANSOM THEORY

When the Fathers began to think of the effect the work and gift of Christ had had on the environment in which man lived, they speculated in terms of a ransom paid to redeem mankind from evil powers. Irenaeus speaks of our having to be redeemed not only from corruption but from the tyranny of 'the apostasy', i.e., satanic power. The powers of evil are regarded as having a legal claim to exercise this tyranny over mankind, for God in paying the price of our redemption does not use violent means, but acts justly, in a persuasive way. Through his wisdom he overcomes the powers of evil. The price he pays is Christ's flesh and blood. 'The Lord thus has redeemed us through his own blood, giving his soul for our souls, and his flesh for our flesh' (*Against Heresies*, 5:1:1).

These ideas were developed by *Origen* (*c*. 185–254), *Gregory of Nyssa* (*c.* 330–394) and others.[10] They speculated that God had laid a trap for the devil. He had made a bargain with him in order to ensnare him. Christ had been the bait. God had offered the devil power over his Son if he would let humanity go free. The offer had been greedily accepted, for it had appealed to the evil one's inordinate pride. Moreover, the valuable prize was the more tempting because it looked as if it could be easily mastered. But having let go of humanity to lay hold of Christ, the devil found he had been duped and caught – like a mouse in a trap or fish on a hook – for ultimate destruction. For he could not hold Christ, who was sinless. He found himself utterly mastered by the Son of God, and condemned for his false accusations.

In this way, as Augustine says, 'the devil was conquered when he thought himself to have conquered, that is, "when Christ was slain".' Augustine adds that since he was conquered 'not by the might of God but by his righteousness . . . so also men, imitating Christ, should seek to conquer the devil by righteousness, not by might' (*On the Trinity*, XIII: xv, xiii).

THE CROSS AS A SACRIFICE AND A DEMONSTRATION OF LOVE

The early church also developed the doctrine of Christ's death as a satisfaction for sin. It had to wait for its fullest expression by Anselm in the eleventh century, but Athanasius can speak of Christ as offering the 'sacrifice of his own body' – 'Offering his own temple and bodily instrument as a substitute for the life of all (he) satisfied all that was required by His death' (*Incarnation*, §§ 10, 9).

The doctrine was gradually developed, especially by the Latin Fathers such as *Tertullian* (*c.* 160–225), *Hilary* (c. 315–368) and *Ambrose* (c. 339–395), and it is expressed often by Augustine, to whom Christ is the 'true sacrifice . . . due to the one true God' (*Trinity*, IV. xiv).

We find in Augustine too a powerful expression of the doctrine that later became so central, as we shall see, to Abelard. 'That the great reason for the advent of Christ was the commendation of love', was a chapter heading of his little treatise *On the Catechising of the Uninstructed*. Augustine quotes the texts, 'While we were yet sinners Christ died for us,' and 'He first loved us,' remarking that there is no mightier invitation to love than to anticipate the loving: 'the love which before was torpid is excited as soon as it feels itself to be loved.' 'Therefore it was mainly for this purpose that Christ came, to wit, that man might learn how much God loves him; and that he might learn this, to the intent that he might be kindled to the love of him by whom he was first loved, and might also love his neighbour' (IV. 7, 8).

THE CLAIM TO COMPREHENSIVENESS – ANSELM AND ABELARD

The church's thought on the atonement developed so quietly and slowly that not until the eleventh century did the preaching current on the subject begin to offend thinking minds. Counter theories began to create controversy. *Anselm* (*c*. 1033–1109) seems to have been the first to take such offence, and to give further offence by producing a new, comprehensive theory in his work *Cur Deus Homo*, which is brief and easily read.

Anselm was deeply dissatisfied with the view that Christ's death was a ransom paid to the devil. There was no reason, he argues in *Cur Deus Homo*, why God should resort to such trickery as the theory suggested. Why should he not use his strength directly, and take a much simpler way? Anselm left the devil out of consideration and saw the problem as entirely a matter between man and God. In face of the enormity of human sin, how can forgiveness be justified and man restored?

For Anselm it was the personal wound inflicted by man on God that created the immensely difficult, urgent problem. He regarded even the least sin, such as a misdirected glance taken contrary to the will of God, as a matter of infinite gravity because it was committed against God. He thought of God and man as dealing with each other within a situation similar to that between the Lord and his vassal under the feudal system of his day. Man is the subject who owes honour and due service to his divine master. But man's disobedience has deprived God of the honour due to him. Man is therefore hopelessly in debt, and powerless to avert judgment – an endless punishment which even in its fulfilment could bring no proper reparation for what man has done. Yet it would be inconsistent with God's glory if he simply forgave man in an arbitrary way.

There is an alternative which maintains his glory and allows him to take man back. God's honour can be maintained if a satisfaction is offered – a satisfaction exceeding the value of the whole universe – as great as the debt of man has been grievous. Only man could interpose and offer such a satisfaction in man's place, for man ought to render it. But only God could give something of greater value than that which is not God. The work of satisfaction must be that of God as man, the work of one who is truly both God and man.

This is why Christ came as he did. Of course he offered to God, in the first place, the perfect life of obedience due to him from all rational beings, but in addition, without owing God any further obedience, he freely gave himself up to death, accepting the consequences of sin. Since he himself was sinless, the God-man was under no obligation to die. He died of his own free will. The endurance of death by such a divine person for God's sake far outweighs all the sins of men, and renders to God everything required to restore his honour.

Moreover, the death of the God-man wins from the Father a store of infinite merit to avail for all mankind. What can God now give his Son who has everything – except to forgive and receive his brethren? On our part, the death endured for us must be received not only as a gift but as an example of how, under all the pressures of life, those who follow him must seek to live to the honour of God and to render to him all that is due.

Such is a summary of Anselm's theory. It has been pointed out that passages in Augustine and in Gregory the Great (*c.* 540–604) show how the thought of Anselm's predecessors was moving towards such a theory.[11] But Anselm's book was of immense influence in opening up new avenues for others, and in spite of its defects it has still many lessons on its subject to teach us today. It raises the most important issues. We will discuss three aspects of its teaching.

Anselm speaks of the *necessity* of the death of Christ. He has been criticised sometimes because he is thought to have paved the way for theories of the atonement which say that what God *has* to do to put things right is preconditioned according to rational principles. But in *Cur Deus Homo*, Anselm insists that the necessity about which he is speaking is a 'sequent' necessity, 'improperly' called 'necessity' (II:18, 5). It arises not out of the nature of things as our human minds can conceive them but out of the nature of God as he has revealed himself to be. It is a necessity which does not compel the atonement to take place but which is deduced from the nature of the work itself. When we look at the cross and realise the effort and sacrifice expended there – its cost to God – we are bound, unless we insult God's wisdom, to understand that only a strange, pressing necessity could lie behind what has been done (I:6).

Anselm stresses what Christ does as man acting towards God. This is in contrast to the ransom theory, which tends to emphasise what God does through the instrumentality of Christ's human nature. In discussing this, Anselm brings out the voluntary nature of Christ's response to God (110).[12] For Anselm, Christ's work as man has been given infinite value through his participation in the divine nature.

Moreover, when Anselm speaks of 'satisfaction' he is thinking of personal as much as public satisfaction.[13] It is a matter of what satisfies the honour of God regarded as a person to whom we owe absolute loyalty, rather than as an impartial administrator concerned with public law and order. What is at stake is not the exact requirements of justice but God's glory. 'Anselm nowhere speaks of God as inflicting punishment on Christ.'[14] What Christ renders to God brings personal tribute and in some way touches his heart. Instead of arguing 'this punishment balances out in weight that which was due to all of us', Anselm argues, 'This life was more deserving of love than are sins hateful' (*Cur Deus Homo*, II.14).

To fully understand Anselm we must imagine the atonement as taking place, not within the framework of public law, but rather within the framework of the feudal loyalty that was so important in his day. His theory cannot be called one of vicarious punishment, and he avoids the quantitative discussion arising out of the necessity of exacting equivalent suffering from a substitute. He offers us a key which he believes will open up for us the mystery of the atonement as far as it can be understood. His work gives the impression that it is not an addition to the current theory but an exclusive substitute for it.

Abelard (1079–1142) soon came along with another theory he thought much better. He criticised Anselm as severely as Anselm had criticised those who spoke of a ransom paid to the devil. A God, he argued, who could be 'in any way delighted with the death of the innocent, or who would find acceptable the death of his Son', could only be regarded as 'cruel and unjust'.[15] Our greatest fault, according to Abelard, was our ignorance of God and our blindness to his love. The purpose of Christ's life and death was to open our eyes and instruct us. He sought to cure us by adopting our nature, living, teaching, praying, dying for us, thus persevering to the uttermost in instructing us by word and deed. This is the proof of God's highest love towards us. It is meant to kindle in our hearts such a response of love as will change us, unite us to God, and constitute the ground of our forgiveness. Justice will demand that Christ's prayer for us should be answered with this result.[16]

Abelard was concerned to safeguard the moral value and influence of Christ's work, and to avoid theories that he felt were too transactional. But in his exposition the atoning work of Christ is made entirely dependent ultimately on our human response. Abelard erred as Anselm had done in suggesting that his view gave a comprehensive account of Christ's work, and in excluding other views. Much of what he said is true, and Augustine had said much of it before him, but without preoccupation with this one aspect. His fault, says Franks, lay in his 'attempt to reduce the whole work of Christ to a single thought'.[17]

6 Later developments

Though there was controversy on the matter of atonement, no councils were called to restrain anybody or to define orthodoxy. When we read the *Summa Theologica* of *Thomas Aquinas* (1224–1274) we realise that here a theologian seeks to say 'both . . . and', where Anselm and Abelard were inclined to say, 'either . . . or'.

When discussing the death of Christ he poses a series of questions asking whether Christ's passion operated by way of sacrifice; whether it brought about our salvation by way of redemption; whether it delivers from sin, or from the devil's power, or from the punishment of sin; whether it reconciled us to God, and opened the gate of heaven. To all these questions Aquinas answers an unswerving Yes. (III. 48–9).

Harnack accuses Thomas of wavering between differing points of view, and of failing to convey any 'distinct impression'. But Thomas gave himself a difficult task. He culled from what his predecessors had said about the cross whatever had a ring of truth, conserving what was good, and criticising and correcting where he could.[1]

Anselm had stressed that God acted under the necessity of maintaining his honour. Thomas discusses whether it was necessary for Christ to suffer, and affirms that it was not necessary in any other sense than that God willed to save men this way. He discourages us from thinking of God as a judge who is under compulsion to punish where punishment is due. 'God has no one higher than himself . . . consequently if he forgives sin . . . he wrongs no one' (Summa, III: 46:2). God, he believes, is in a position to do other than he does. Yet Thomas admits that it was fitting for Christ to die, and that it is a fitting way of satisfying for another, to submit oneself to the penalty deserved by the other (III: 50:1).

Thomas also tries to preserve the best in the thought of Abelard. 'Many things,' he writes, 'besides deliverance from sin concurred for man's salvation. In the first place through it [Christ's passion] man knows how much God loves him, and is thereby stirred up to love him in return, and herein lies the perfection of human salvation' (III: 46:3).

Seeing the cross as a revelation of love aroused within him, as it had within many in the Middle Ages, deep sensibility to the physical sufferings the human Jesus underwent in his passion. But Aquinas sees that Jesus' whole life constituted his passion, and involved him in every imaginable human affliction. He discusses how deeply Jesus must have felt the behaviour of his friends, the crowds mocking, and the people refusing to believe (III: 46:5–7).

Thomas regards Christ's passion as an aspect of his obedience and a contribution to his work of satisfaction. He sees his inner love and grief as redemptive: 'By suffering out of love and obedience Christ gave more to God than was required to compensate for the whole offence of the human race . . . because of the exceeding charity from which he suffered' (III: 47:2; 48:2). Moreover, because of 'the dignity of his life . . . the extent of the passion and the greatness of the grief endured', Christ's passion was not only a sufficient but a 'super-abundant' atonement for the sins of the human race (III: 48:2).

All this develops Anselm's idea that Christ's divinity gives infinite value to the sufferings of the God-man. Certainly the thought of a 'super-abundant' atonement lifts the whole subject, at least for a moment, out of the realm of discussing equivalents.

Under headings of the efficiency and merit of Christ's sufferings Thomas raises, again, the issue important for Athanasius and Irenaeus, and to become so important for Calvin: that in Christ 'the head and the members are as one mystic person; and therefore Christ's satisfaction belongs to all the faithful as being his members.' 'Grace,' he says, 'was bestowed on Christ, not only as an individual, but inasmuch as he is the head of the church, so that it might overflow into his members' (III: 48:1, 2).

Of course there is much in Thomas that Luther and Calvin had to reject, but they profited enormously from him. He tried to hold everything together, and to develop the thought of those who had gone before him. Franks points out that 'nowhere can the real problems of theology be better studied, by anyone who has sufficient patience, than in the mediaeval scholasticism.'[2]

Whereas Thomas Aquinas' theology is an aggregate of many distinct ingredients, Franks describes *Luther*'s theology as a 'higher form of organism in which the whole is in every part and every part is in the whole'.[3] Luther manages to say many things when he says one thing. Yet he too varies his emphasis. As Kostlin says, 'We find him presenting now one, now another feature of the subject, just as the immediate occasion may suggest, and particularly as his mind is influenced from time to time by the passages of Scripture which he may be seeking to elucidate.'[4]

Luther continually pleads for the integration of our experience and our theology. What has been achieved by Christ once for all must be re-actualised here and now within the life of the Christian. This process will help us to understand and interpret the atonement. Luther *felt* the cross as vividly as he *saw* the cross. He believed his own experience under the cross was similar to what others should feel, and he expected others to share it with him.

He was content to think of the meaning of the cross in terms of the simple pictures the Bible provides when it speaks of the work of Christ. 'We must . . . conceive of *all* things which we cannot understand and know, in pictures, even though they may not actually be just as the pictures represent them. I propose to keep close to the pictures, for with lofty thoughts and keen questions, the devil would easily draw me off the track.'[5] Three of these pictures were central in his thought – Christ in our conflict, Christ offering an exchange with us, Christ bearing and overcoming the wrath of God for us.

Christ in our conflict

Luther often pictures the devil as being overcome by Christ. He speaks of Christ coming to 'catch the devil' and of the latter being enticed with bait and so deceived. He is repeating in detail the old-fashioned theory of Christ given as a ransom to the devil (*LW* 5:150; 53:220; 51:62). But he often personifies the law and conceives it as the enemy of both man and God (40:417; 26:370).[6] For Luther 'it is Christ's true and proper function to struggle with the law and sin and death of the entire world, and to struggle in such a way that he undergoes them, but by undergoing conquers them and abolishes them in himself, thus liberating us from the law and every evil.' Often Luther imagines sin and death as well as the law assailing Christ and almost overcoming, only to be utterly shattered in the end (26:373; 280–1).

Luther, in describing Christ's struggle in these ways, is also describing his own well-known inner struggles. Paul Althaus points out that, for Luther, the evil powers still rule the world and fight against the church and Christendom. Therefore 'Christ now wages battle in the hearts of Christians by word and sacrament.' Luther speaks too of Christ's victory having its beginnings in the hearts of believers. 'He who once rose from the dead, constantly and unceasingly rises from the dead in his Christians.'[7]

The wonderful exchange

Christ was innocent so far as his own person was concerned, Luther asserted. He should not have been hanged. But 'Christ himself should have been hanged, for he bore the person of a sinner and a thief – and not of one, but of all sinners and thieves.' Luther speaks of Christ as standing in our place and taking our sins on his shoulders, bearing our sins (*LW* 26:277; 51:92; 12:365).

> Jesus Christ, God's only Son
> In our place descending
> Away with all our sins hath done. (*LW* 53:257).

He speaks also of Christ being 'the eternal satisfaction for our sins', a term he frequently uses (though he regarded it as inadequate) in connection with the requirements of God's honour and justice (51:92).[8]

Christ bears our sins in our place so that he can make an exchange with us. In his ninety-five theses he calls this 'the most pleasant participation in the benefits of Christ, and joyful change of life'.[9] 'He took upon himself our sinful person and granted us his innocent and victorious person.' 'What is ours becomes his, and what is his becomes ours' (*LW* 26:284, 292).

This seems to echo Athanasius and Irenaeus and Augustine. But these Fathers were almost wholly concerned with what took place through the incarnation. Luther, on the other hand, seems at times to have a double reference. When he describes the 'wonderful exchange', where 'one man has peace coming to him, and another man receives it,' he is thinking of a transaction between Christ and a living individual believer (*WA* 31:435). For Luther, as Kostlin says, 'whatever Christ . . . accomplished for us is now by virtue of his working in us, to find a copy in our own lives and conduct.'[10] This happens by faith, as we make ourselves one with Christ. 'Christ is full of grace, life and salvation. The soul is full of sins, death and damnation. Now let faith come between them, and sins, death and damnation will be Christ's, while grace, life and salvation will be the soul's' (*LW* 31:351).

Christ and the wrath of God

Luther felt that the word 'satisfaction' inadequately expressed the significance of Christ's work, but he did describe Christ as the 'eternal satisfaction for our sin', who reconciles us with God.[11] He speaks of such satisfaction as a payment in accordance with divine justice, and rendered to God's honour and justice.[12] More often, however, Christ, in his battle with the evil powers, deals directly with the 'wrath of God', for Luther sees powers such as the law, death, and the devil as strangely having the 'wrath of God' on their side.[13]

Luther gives the 'wrath of God' a position subordinate to his love, and, indeed, of service to his love. 'God is good, righteous and merciful even when he strikes.' For love is 'the most precious and perfect virtue in God and man'.[14] But God is 'the eternal righteousness and purity who by his very nature hates sin'.[15] If God's righteousness expresses itself in a work of wrath, this is an alien work, against his nature. Wrath is not an essential part of God's being as in the case of love and righteousness – though we sometimes wrongly imagine it to be. His wrath is the 'wrath of mercy', though when it visits us it has a *dreadful reality*. We imagine it to be the wrath of severity because of our sinfulness.[16]

When we are alienated from God his 'wrath' brings us under conviction of sin with the terrors of an alarmed conscience. This was fully felt by Christ as he stood before God in our place, 'clothed in our person', having become a sinner worthy of the wrath of God, and uttering our confession, 'I have committed the sins that all men have committed.'[17] He who had no sin became the greatest murderer, and blasphemer – sin itself. 'Whatever sins you and I and all or us have committed or may commit in the future, they are as much Christ's own as if he himself had committed them' (*LW* 26:280, 283, 278).

Luther sees the cries and confessions of the psalmists in their deep sense of sin as literally Christ's cries and confessions, pleading and in agony under the wrath of God.[18] Jesus' cry of dereliction, the echo of Psalm 22 – 'my God, my God why hast thou forsaken me?' – he sees as his deepest utterance of agony, and affirms that this is our clue for understanding the clause in the creed: 'He descended into hell.' Luther spoke of Jesus at this point as being abandoned by God, allowed to rest under the guilt of sin; indeed, left momentarily in the hands of the devil. He experienced 'eternal terrors and torments' as he felt the hellish fire. God assumed the attitude of an enemy and struck him.[19]

Luther's interpretation of the descent into hell was original. Even Thomas Aquinas in his attempt to understand the sufferings of Christ had not probed this aspect.[20] This part of Luther's teaching was followed by Calvin, but not by his own followers. His doctrine of the cross, says Althaus, 'transcends all earlier theology through the radical seriousness with which he allows Christ to suffer both hell and being totally forsaken by God'.[21]

Discussing Christ before the wrath of God, Luther finds even there an analogy between Christ's passion and the temptation and despair which the godly experience, each in his own conscience. God allows each of us, like Job and Jacob, to go through 'a repetition of the sufferings of Jesus in his abandonment by God'.[22] Christ's death is, for Luther, an example of how we should bear the despair and judgment we feel as we allow ourselves to be drawn into the fellowship of Christ's sufferings. Following Augustine, he refers to Christ's death as a sacrament that proclaims our spiritual death, slays the former and awakens the new man within us.[23]

In his early writings the objective and subjective aspects of Christ's work are at times so fused that it seems that the objective work found its realisation only when this spiritual crucifixion took place. But later he stressed the sheer priority of the objective work: our victory is achieved through the proclamation of Christ's victory, and as Christ lives and reigns within us.[24]

Moving on, we have to note a very important development at this stage of the church's thought about the atonement. Aquinas had said that in so far as any two men are in charity, the one can atone for the other, and he had discussed how the merit of one can avail for another (*Summa*, III: 48:3). Luther swept away all ideas of such meriting on our part. But boldly and in a new way he insisted that we can, as Christians within the fellowship of Christ and the church, bear the sins of each other. This point is put strongly in his remarkable early treatise on the participation in the body and blood of Christ.[25] In an early letter to George Spenlein he pleads that 'just as Christ has made your sins his own . . . receive your untaught and hitherto erring brothers, patiently help them, make their sins yours, and, if you have any goodness, let it be theirs' (*LW* 48:12–13).

Luther does not mean that we can do for each other what Christ did in taking away our guilt. He means the kind of heart burden of the prophets and apostles that found expression in intercessory prayers. And Luther warns, 'You should accustom yourself to distinguish carefully between the suffering of Christ and all other suffering, and know that his is a heavenly suffering and ours is worldly, that his suffering accomplishes everything, while ours does nothing except that we became conformed to the sufferings of Christ' (*LW* 51:208).

Aquinas too had differentiated clearly 'the part of Christ's sufferings which a man can endure', and those that were unique to himself (*summa*, III: 46:5). Yet at times Luther interpreted even Christ's vicarious sufferings as being due significantly to his human sympathy. Kostlin quotes him as saying, 'Although that is compassion (*compassio*) and not actual suffering (*passio*), nevertheless that compassion was without doubt a great part of the whole of the sufferings of Christ.'[26] Kostlin concludes: 'Luther then finds even to the very culminating point of the Saviour's sufferings, as an essential element and even as the chief element, a feeling of sympathy for us analogous to our sympathy for one another.' This aspect of the atonement was taken up by Jonathan Edwards (see pp. 97f.), and is at the centre of much modern thinking on the subject.

When we turn to *Calvin* our impression is one of order. Even where things cannot fit together they are at least placed in better view. Everything important is here, from every source. It is as if someone has marvellously tidied up a house incredibly full of stuff that seemed junk when viewed in its mess, put everything in place and disposed of nothing of any value.

Calvin believed that the incarnation took place only because we had sinned, and devotes one or two paragraphs of the *Institutes*[27] to discussing this (2:12:4 ff); but before he does so, in three short introductory sections he gives his own version of *Cur Deus Homo* (2:12:1–3).

We can compare him with Anselm and see how far he has advanced. Why did our salvation take the form it did? Calvin does not picture a feudal ruler or a judge of mankind concerned about the order of the universe. He turns to other aspects of the Creator – wisdom and love. It was what was best for us; and 'he was moved by pure and freely given love' (2:12:1. 2:16:3). For Calvin one problem is much more acute than any legal problem – it is our estrangement from God our Father who created us to live at his side. The need, then, in our atonement is to recreate 'a nearness near enough and an affinity sufficiently firm for us to hope that God might dwell with us.' We needed an incarnation to save us, not just a cross. In becoming flesh, God comes to us in such a way that 'his divinity and our human nature might by mutual connection grow together'. However, restoration of our union with God cannot take place unless the mediator is a man entering a 'holy brotherhood' with us under the one Father. But only God in coming close to us could 'swallow up death and replace it with life, conquer sin and replace it with righteousness' (2:12:1–2). At this point Calvin is following closely Irenaeus and Athanasius.

In the third paragraph of this short, pregnant introduction, he writes of how Christ reversed the disobedience of Adam and, clothed in our flesh, vanquished death; but he also speaks of him as offering 'a satisfaction to God's righteous judgment', and appeasing 'the Father's righteous wrath' very much in the same language as Luther.[28] All this must be seen as enclosed in the Fatherhood of God who gave us his Son because he wants us back (*Inst.* 2:12:3).

Calvin develops the latter aspect of Christ's death in his discussion of the fulfilment of his priestly office before God (2:15:6). Still closely following Luther, he shows how a participation in the mediating work of Christ is open to ourselves. Jesus is continuing his priestly office as an 'everlasting intercessor . . . not only to render the Father favourable and propitious towards us . . . but to receive us as companions in his great office.'

Later Calvin discusses the work of Christ in an exposition of the clauses of the Creed: 'suffered under Pontius Pilot, was crucified, dead, and buried. He descended into hell.' Christ's whole early life is described by the words, 'He suffered'. It follows that at the very beginning of his human life Jesus 'began to pay the price of our liberation' (2:16:5), and that his whole life of obedience is part of his offering for our salvation.

Aquinas had brought out time and again how the meaning and effects of Christ's passion were shown in the 'very manner of his death' (*Summa*, III: 47:4) – many of its concrete details were 'fitting' and allegorically significant. Similarly, Calvin reads the doctrine from the actual historical picture. That Jesus the man was legally condemned, though innocent, before Pontus Pilate, gave a sign that in another world of reality too he bore not his own, but the sins of others. Any other kind of violent death could not have given this evidence. Calvin points out, as Paul did, that to be 'crucified' is a form of death which also 'embodies a singular mystery'. It means that he 'took God's curse' as a 'sacrificial victim' in order to give blessing and to wash away corruption (*Inst.* 2:16:5–6).

When discussing his being 'dead and buried', Calvin echoes the old theory about the deceit played on the devil. 'He let himself be swallowed up by death, as it were, not to be engulfed in its abyss, but, rather, to engulf it.' In this way the devil too was overcome. Since it was a point of controversy, Calvin spends some time arguing that Christ's descent into hell meant his dereliction on the cross (2:16:7–12). In this chapter Calvin has many things to say about Jesus' suffering God's wrath and the penalty for our sins, but here again he is careful to preface everything he says by insisting that the work of atonement derives from God's love (2:16:3–4).

THE SEVENTEENTH-CENTURY DEFINITION OF PENAL SUBSTITUTION

In the seventeenth century one particular aspect of Christ's work on the cross received an almost exclusive priority. This was how Christ 'by his perfect obedience and sacrifice of himself . . . fully satisfied the justice of his father.'[29] We have a situation defined where legal demands tend to be paramount. God, as judge, is bound to act in accordance with so-called principles of absolute justice. Justice, to be satisfied, demands the retributive punishment of those who break the law. Even God is not in a position to ignore this demand. In exercising his fatherly mercy, forgiving us sinners, the debt to justice has to be paid and the punishment exacted. Christ is therefore called, and offers in our stead a life of perfect obedience in response to God's law. God accepts him as a substitute and representative, and, transferring on to him the whole sin and guilt of those who are spared, punishes him with a punishment meet for those who have been spared. This brings complete satisfaction, and we can be forgiven.

This theory was expounded within a theology which regarded Christ as fulfilling his mediatorial offices of prophet, priest and king. The work of reconciliation was seen as belonging largely to his priestly ministry. Theologians disagreed about how the human and the divine natures shared the task, but they did mostly agree that Christ's whole life was effective in bringing about the atonement, and that both his active and passive obedience had integral rôles in the work – his active obedience being his perfect fulfilment of the law; his passive obedience being his willing acceptance of the punishment and curse of the law. His obedience had won merit which can be transferred to us in the Father's sight.

It is easy to argue that the writings of both Luther and Calvin helped the rise of this theory, but this is to overlook much of what they wrote and to select only those passages where they deal with the penal aspect of the atonement. This is exactly what their successors did, and the result is what is called 'Protestant scholasticism'.

Calvin's style was clear. He liked brevity, his thinking was orderly. In his *Institutes* he tried to arrange and expound each doctrine in the light of the whole revelation of God in Christ. He tried also to relate the logic of his theology to a divine logic he found in revelation itself, and to cast off the logic of the human mind. Within his attempt at a unified system he purposely introduced things that confounded all our logic, and he avoided working with any one central principle. But Calvin's immediate follower, *Beza*, re-arranged the system taught in

Geneva so as to give the doctrine of predestination the priority Calvin had tried to avoid. Also, his followers were more concerned than their great predecessor strictly to follow the rules of human logic in their theological discourse. They sought to clarify all the mysteries of faith by precisely detailed discussion. Many shared the feeling of Richard Baxter who confessed, 'I could never from my first studies endure confusion. I never thought I understood anything till I could anatomise it and see its parts distinctly, and the conjunction of the parts as they make up the whole.'[30]

It was not surprising, then, that they clarified the work done in the atonement by selecting the one aspect that could be most easily understood. The effect of giving the doctrine of predestination a dominant place led to the assertion that the atonement was limited in its scope – sometimes called the doctrine of a particular or limited atonement, in contrast to the doctrine of a universal atonement. Christ, it was asserted, died only for the elect. This was an assertion Calvin had never seriously discussed, but it now became important in reformed circles.

They tended to over-develop when teaching. A typical example is *Thomas Goodwin*'s careful distinction between Christ being made 'sin' and made a 'curse'. The one, he says, was by imputation; the other by infliction, i.e., Christ in being made sin did not know what it was to sin, but in being made a curse he knew it – to his cost. The curse had two aspects: that which arose out of judicial law, and that which arose from moral law.[31]

In their zeal to drive home their points they tended, perhaps in imitation of Luther's rhetoric, to slip into a phraseology that needlessly offended and was bound to arouse opposition. Expounding the doctrine of satisfaction, Stephen Charnock writes of God's attitude to Christ: 'He was desirous to hear him groaning, and see him bleeding . . . He refused not to strike him that he might be well pleased with us; quenched his sword in the blood of his son that it might be for ever wet.'[32] Likewise, Goodwin speaks of God as letting justice 'fly upon' Christ, 'to have its full pennyworth out of him. He lets wrath suck the blood of his soul, till it falls off, as the leech when it is filled and breaks.'[33] Where Luther spoke eloquently, rhetorically and effectively about all our sins being laid on Christ, Goodwin writes of him 'being made a common drain and sink into which all the sins of every particular man do run, and the centre in which they all meet; and that meeting implies an assembly of particular sins.'[34]

Each and all our sins matter to Christ: to teach this is a rightful pastoral task. But Calvin's followers began to insist that each sin quantitatively added its weight to what Christ bore on Calvary. People began to be suspicious. The way the theory was presented gave difficulties of conception that smacked of unreality.

The first reaction against the penal substitution theory came in the seventeenth century from the followers of *Socinus* (1539–1604). They were outside the pale of orthodoxy anyway, but may have been driven further into heresy by their dislike of what the orthodox preached. Christ, to the Socinians, was merely a prophet whose teaching was confirmed by his resurrection. They raised many objections which they regarded as reasonable. God's will, they asserted, was above the law of justice which was merely the effect of God's will. If a human being can pardon without satisfaction, why not God? Anyway, to impose a penalty on an innocent could not be justice but torture. They asserted that satisfaction and pardon were incompatible, and that it was impossible to fit the idea of substitution into a conception of true justice.[35]

Within orthodox circles some of these objections were raised by the Arminians.[36] However their main objection was to the idea of limited atonement. *Grotius* (1583–1645) deserves mention. He was an Arminian who, to avoid the idea that God had to exact from Christ equivalent penal satisfaction, suggested that the death of Christ was to be understood as an example of rectoral justice. Christ was executed as a substitute because an example of public justice helps to maintain good government in the universe.

The Puritan theologians who defended their doctrine of penal substitution and limited atonement against such attacks were undoubtedly men of great virtues, deep religious experience, and they could preach with heart-warming eloquence. *John Owen* (1618–1688) strikingly compares the cross to Noah's ark.

> When the flood fell there were many mountains, glorious to the eye, far higher than the ark; but yet the mountains were all drowned, whilst the ark still kept on the top of the waters. Many appearing hills and mountains of self-righteousness and general mercy, at the first view, seem to the soul much higher than Jesus Christ, but when the flood of wrath once comes and spreads itself, all these mountains are quickly covered; only the ark, the Lord Jesus Christ, though the flood fall on him also, yet he gets above it quite, and gives safety to those that rest on him.

In the midst of the flood he compares our poor soul to the bird released by Noah, looking for a resting place but perceiving only 'an ocean, a flood, an inundation of wrath . . . heaven itself it cannot reach by its own flight and to hell it is unwilling to fall . . . Alas, what shall it do? . . . if the Lord Jesus Christ do not appear as an ark in the midst of the waters.'

Owen in conclusion utters an appeal from the soul itself: 'Bereave me of the satisfaction of Christ and I am bereaved. If he fulfilled not justice I must; if he underwent not wrath I must to eternity. O rob me not of my only peace.'[37] Yet Owen argued unswervingly and powerfully that Christ did not die for all mankind. For him it was against logic to admit that a ransom could be paid for captives who were not thereby free. Having rejected the Arminian doctrine of freedom of the will, he argued that if God willed all men to be saved they would thereby be saved. It would make Christ only a half-mediator if he 'procured the end but not the means conducting thereto'. Christ therefore satisfied for no more souls than he intended actually to save. Owen is arguing from the viewpoint that somehow the amount of satisfaction rendered to God can be evaluated to cover the elect and no others, and that the number saved must tally with something already done by Christ.[38] He insisted that Christ paid a 'full valuable compensation' for all the sins of those for whom he made satisfaction, and explained this equivalence as 'the same in weight and pressure, though not in all accidents of duration and the like'.[39]

NINETEENTH-CENTURY CONTRIBUTIONS

In the eighteenth century several important new thoughts were developed. For example in America, where Grotius' theories had a strong influence, *Jonathan Edwards* (1703–1758) raised psychological questions which perhaps only Luther had asked before, about the sufferings of Jesus as a human person, especially allowing for his sympathy as an important ingredient. He asked, Could a perfect repentance have been offered by the Mediator to God rather than his having to undergo substitutionary punishment? – and rejected his own provocative suggestion. *Bishop Butler* (1692–1752) in England in his famous *Analogy of Religion* pointed out that Scripture itself does not explain the working of the atonement, and he pleaded for it to be accepted, like sacrifice in the Old Testament, as a mystery. He remarked that 'vicarious punishment was a providential appointment of every day's experience.'[40]

These were individual, valuable insights, but it was in the nineteenth century that fresh discussion took place on the doctrine of the atonement which led to a deepening of the church's understanding of the cross. The discussion was part of the general movement of theology dominated on the Continent by Schleiermacher and Kant, and in Britain by Coleridge and Erskine.

One of the most important contributions was made by a Scotsman, *J. McLeod Campbell* (1800–1872) in *The Nature of the Atonement*.[41] Campbell lays down conditions which a satisfactory doctrine of the atonement must fulfil: We must feel that what was offered to God was really due from ourselves, that it was impossible for us to render it, and yet we must be able to have its elements reproduced within us. We must, however, learn from the atonement itself why it was needed, and how it could fill this need, and we must lay down no other prior conditions. The Gospel must be allowed to cast its own light on the subject (pp. 294, 228).

At the centre of the Gospel there is the Fatherhood of God. Campbell felt that the stress on God as the judge, the concern to obtain legal remission and the imputation of Christ's righteousness, did not encourage men and women in his day to look to the Father and receive the Spirit of sonship, entering a life of living piety and prayer. How much better to evangelise by appealing to people to receive the Spirit of sonship inspired by faith in the Father's gracious invitation, than to try to move them to come to God with confidence because they supposed themselves to be clothed with legal righteousness! 'We must come to God as sons, or not at all' (pp. 172, 348–9).

The great Dr Chalmers had expressed his fear of the sentimental piety of the time; he believed the sinner must be awakened by the thought of God as judge. 'Let us guard against awakenings,' wrote Campbell, 'that do not reach the depth of man's being' (p. 72).

Campbell disliked the idea of Christ coming to fulfil an office as mediator according to a pre-arranged plan. This encouraged the view of his life as unnatural – a mere 'scenic representation'. We must understand what Jesus came to do in the light of what was ultimately accomplished – our union with himself, our receiving the Son as our true life in whom we can call God Father, with an intimate understanding of what sonship means. Legal terms are not appropriate. The central problem is not, how can sinners be pardoned? but how can we, God's offspring, being dead, be made alive again, being lost become found? (pp. 230, 364, 92).

Criticising the penal theory, Campbell found that nowhere was suffering demanded by God in Scripture. The reign of law as such, he stated, 'affords no place for atonement as indeed it offers no place for prayer'. Christ's sufferings, he asserted, were not penal. His pain was 'pain endured in sympathy with God,' and in the strength of the faith of the divine acceptance of that sympathy. 'Surely the tears of a godly parent over a prodigal are not penal.' The sufferings of Christ are unique because of their intensity, not because of their measurable quantity (pp. 292, xliv, 133, 117, 139–40). In any case forgiveness, he argued, is prior to the atonement, which is the manifestation of forgiving love. We must avoid the error of representing the Son as exercising an influence on the Father to make him gracious (pp. 18, 20, 229).

Campbell urges us to see God's love revealed not just in connection with the atonement but within it. The divine fatherhood itself is revealed in the sonship of the Son. Yet Campbell rejected the Abelardian view. The atonement is there because there was something necessarily to be done, a redemption to be achieved only at great cost (pp. 141, 24, 26).

Jonathan Edwards had said that there must be 'either an equivalent punishment or an equivalent sorrow and repentance', but he had assumed that the latter was out of the question. Campbell asserts that Edwards pointed out the right direction though he did not himself take it. Christ has actually offered to God this equivalent sorrow and repentance. His oneness of mind with the Father in condemning our sins, and his brotherhood with us were bound to issue in his confessing perfectly to the Father our sins. Jesus uttered 'the *perfect Amen in humanity to the judgment of God on the sins of man*'. And this was the atoning sacrifice demanded by the Father. It is an expiation due not just to the righteous law of God but to the fatherly heart of God (pp. 137, 175, 183).[42] Moreover, in our faith in God's acceptance of this confession on our behalf we ourselves receive strength to say Amen to it, and, joining in it, to 'find a living way to God'. In this way Christ's righteousness becomes ours and is reproduced in us (pp. 182, 159, 177).

Christ's sufferings are such that we can understand them. They were not penal. His cry of dereliction on the cross was not due to his abandonment by God, but expressed his perplexity at being left in the hands of the wicked. Yet he was conscious of God's wrath against sin, and must have suffered more deeply from his sympathy with it. His death was more bitter than ours could ever be. Since he was sinless, life to him was more desirable than it could be to any other being. Therefore he 'tasted death' in its full contrast to eternal life. Knowing the mind of God against sin, he regarded it as the wages of sin (pp. 319, 277, 230, 290–1, 302).

That we can in some way understand Christ's sufferings means that we can in some way suffer with Christ and enter his confession of our sins. Christ's own sense of our sin and his hope for us made him intercede for us in an appeal to his Father's heart which was perfectly responded to. Therefore Christ's confession of our sins was necessarily supplemented by his intercession for us. This intercession was the natural and perfect form of his sacrifice (pp. 319, 231-2, 234). It was an intent, earnest and agonising prayer that we might have eternal life, and it was answered. In sharing Christ's sonship and sufferings we ourselves share in this intercession. The atonement revealed one of the laws of the kingdom of God: prayer is answered. In prayer we influence God, not to make him gracious but because he *is* gracious (pp. xxxi, 228). God is free to grant what we ask.

Far from being less severe morally than the penal doctrine, Campbell claims that his doctrine is actually more so. He speaks of the 'high capacity for good' in human nature when it becomes related to the Son of God. It is there hidden under sin, but not hidden from God, and is brought forth by Christ (pp. 188 ff). The new relation between the Son of God and the sins of men is that of a quickening spirit. Campbell sums up his doctrine:

> Our faith is in truth the Amen of our individual spirits to that deep, multiform, all-embracing, harmonious Amen of humanity, in the person of the Son of God, to the mind and heart of the Father in relation to man – the divine wrath and the divine mercy, which is the atonement (pp. 160, 225).

Contemporary with McLeod Campbell, *F. D. Maurice* (1805–1872) also stressed Christ's self-identifying love for mankind. This, along with his personal divine holiness, was the key to his sufferings, and his surrender to the holy will of God was the key to the satisfaction he offered.

In the United States there appeared the work of *Horace Bushnell* (1802–1876). He did not take as seriously as Maurice or Campbell Christ's abhorrence and condemnation of our sins. He sought to explain the sufferings of the cross as simply due to his love. His central thought is that love is vicarious in its character, and the sacrifice of Christ is its supreme instance. But Christ suffered just as any missionary suffers what belongs to the work of love he is in.[43] Bushnell also held that Christ paid high honour to the law.

The teaching of McLeod Campbell was a needed corrective to the penal substitution theory. He brought out much in the Gospel that had been obscured, and his book is much more impressive than any summary can convey. But his account of the cause and nature of Christ's sufferings does not do full justice to the teaching of the New Testament.

Throughout the nineteenth century many were staunch upholders and preachers of penal substitution, for example T. J. Crawford and G. Smeaton in Britain, and in the United States theologians like Shedd and Hodge. Among the supporters of the theory some, like R. Wardlaw, argued for a universal atonement.

A notable contribution was made by *R. W. Dale* (1829–1895). He criticised the current penal doctrine which seemed to hand over the moral government of the universe to self-acting laws, of which God was an otiose spectator, and where mercy seemed to have no power.[44] For Dale the law was *alive* in God, 'reigns on His throne, sways His sceptre, is crowned with His glory'. It is neither above nor below him, but is embodied in him.[45]

Sin does demand and deserve punishment. Conscience, though it cannot forgive, can bear witness in a terrifying way to the divine law and to our guilt. The facts of life themselves give the same evidence. 'You cannot escape from it. The malignant lie, the act of cruelty, the deliberate dishonesty will cling to you year after year, and you will not by any moral effort be able to throw it off.'[46] Moreover, sin demands retributive punishment – a penalty designed to punish rather than to reform or to satisfy wounded honour in God (*Atonement*, p. 374–7).

Since he is so identified with righteousness, God's judgment becomes the expression of his personal abhorrence of, and anger against, sin. He would cease to be God if he did not thus express the eternal law of righteousness (p. 385). Therefore there is a necessity – for a 'divine act which shall have all the moral worth and significance of the act by which the penalties of sin would have been inflicted on the sinner'. So in the death of Christ, God's hostility to our sins is given an adequate expression.

In thinking of the atonement we must not think of the penalties of sin as held back by the hand of God. God himself asserts 'by his own act, that suffering is the just result of sin'. Yet God asserts this 'not by inflicting suffering upon the sinner, but by enduring suffering himself'. 'The mysterious unity of the Father and the Son rendered it possible for God at once to endure and inflict penal suffering, and to do both under conditions which constitute the infliction and endurance the grandest moment in the moral history of God' (p. 391–3).

Thus where McLeod Campbell and Maurice emphasise the intense sufferings of the human Jesus in the tension created by human sin, Dale, in a remarkably bold way, emphasises the sufferings of God himself in the same tension of holiness and love. This became a common ingredient in twentieth-century thinking.

It should be mentioned that Dale's book is largely a very valuable and detailed exposition of all the New Testament passages relating to the atonement. He also saw clearly that Christ's part was not simply that of an individual substituting for us, but that of representing all humanity. Christ felt he was 'collective mankind' and God saw collective mankind in him (p. 423). Dale speaks of 'the wonderful solidarity' between Christ and the human race. 'Our sin he could not share; but He came into the dark and awful shadow which sin had cast upon the life of men.'[47] The benefits of his death become ours not by imputation but by living communion with him – 'through the law which constitutes his life the original spring of our own' (*Atonement*, p. 422).

Dale insists that Christ's sufferings in the last instance were penal and beyond our capacity. 'The sufferings indeed were His, that they might not be ours; He endured them that we might escape from them.' He interprets the cry of dereliction on the cross to mean that Christ was in reality forsaken by God (p. 431). Yet we now must enter into and share the suffering which he entered in his unique, solitary way. His sacrifice was made for us, but we have a part in it. It was his that it might be made ours, 'though in our inferior form'. We, too, are involved in a 'similar moral act', 'a similar consent to the righteousness of the penalties which we have deserved' (p. 433). Through Christ we can 'retain or recover our original and ideal relation to God' (p. 425).

PART 3

THEOLOGICAL GUIDELINES – THE TWENTIETH-CENTURY DISCUSSION

7 The cross and the incarnate life

CLARIFICATION IN DIVERSITY

The beginning of twentieth-century literature on the atonement can be pinpointed to the appearance of James Denney's *The Death of Christ* (1901) and *The Atonement and the Modern Mind* (1903), and R. C. Moberly's *Atonement and Personality* (1901). Then followed, before the Great War, P. T. Forsyth's *The Cruciality of the Cross* and *The Work of Christ*; also Hastings Rashdall's *The Idea of the Atonement in Christian Theology*. After the first world war came Gustav Aulen's *Christus Victor*, Emil Brunner's *Mediator*, and the works of Karl Heim, later translated under the titles *Jesus the Lord* and *Jesus the World Perfector*. There were the writings of Karl Barth – especially his volumes on *The Doctrine of Reconciliation* in his *Church Dogmatics*. Other writers are referred to in the Notes.

Here are works of lasting value and importance. Thought on the atonement has always developed slowly: new theories have been as rare as the discovery of new planets, and even our great theologians of this century have done little more on the subject than to clarify, modify and restate what others have already said – though in the process they have sometimes given us brilliant new expressions and refined our insights.

Continuing discussion and clarification is essential for us if we are to teach and preach the cross today. We have to estimate for ourselves the trend of thought followed by the church on the atonement; its progress, and where and why it has erred. What past insights are most valuable for us?

In this section we have arranged the more important themes under various headings to provide 'theological guidelines'. A full historical review of the literature would take up too much room, but we believe that some justice can be done through the references and quotations selected because they have something illuminating and important to say. We have to seek as wide a field of discussion as possible. We have to avoid selecting one theory, or one aspect, and giving it undue importance. We cannot afford to neglect any avenue of thought. My own experience of preaching twice a Sunday for many years in the ministry before teaching theology to students has shown me that different biblical texts and stories point us towards quite different aspects of the cross in order to spotlight its significance.

If we are to do full justice to the varying witnesses, and let them fully illuminate the meaning of the Gospel, we shall require now one 'theory' of the atonement and now another to help us in our exposition. Often we shall see some new aspect of the cross that does not quite fit into any kind of dogmatic system at all. We must be prepared for this. We must allow our thinking to be dominated by the shape and dynamic of the biblical text rather than by our theological preferences. The Bible allows us a large area to move in, with many different levels and standpoints from which we can look at the death of Christ. Brunner notes that it was because Luther always ranged himself on the side of the Bible that he switched about constantly in his thinking and exposition from one 'theory' to another, and never found any one at a time sufficient.[1]

THE CROSS, THE INCARNATION AND THE LIFELONG OBEDIENCE OF JESUS

The New Testament writers thought of the incarnation, life, death, resurrection and ascension of Jesus as all together making up one redeeming act or movement of God. For Paul[2] each of these great stages in Jesus' career is to be seen and understood in the light of the others. Jesus' sacrifice is to be seen as beginning with his incarnation. As Emil Brunner says: 'The Passion of Christ . . . does not begin in history at all, but on that mysterious borderline between time and eternity. It begins with the "self-emptying", with the "coming" of Christ. The incarnation should be regarded from the point of view of suffering.'[3]

The cross was already there at the cradle. There were no visible signs of God's eternal majesty about the babe as he lay in the stable. He entered human life as one in whom divine glory was to remain thickly veiled in the 'flesh'. Already at his birth the decisive step had been taken into the shame and misunderstanding, the full humiliation suffered at Calvary. Thomas Goodwin has suggested that since the flesh he assumed was frail, assumption of it can be regarded as 'satisfactory' in the sense that it was an aspect of his atoning work.[4] If, going further than even Goodwin, we decide that he assumed our fallen human nature, this would add an extra dimension to what he entered when he became man.[5]

P. T. Forsyth is right in asking us to see Jesus' earthly life as dominated by a 'premundane volition' that took him finally to the cross. One overwhelming purpose brought him amongst us, and was the driving impulse in all that he did.[6] Though often hidden behind the sympathetic actions of his human love, it nevertheless acted simultaneously.

The apostle John interprets even the details of Jesus' life in the light of his whole movement from God back to God. For instance, his laying aside his garments to wash the disciples' feet is taken as a sign of his original laying aside his glory to come and save us; his stooping is a sign of his entry into human life (John 13:1 ff). In the same way we are justified in interpreting his other loving actions – his laying his hands on children, and on the dead; his stooping to take by the hand the little epileptic boy who had fallen – as moved by the same imperative. They are signs that he, Son of God as well as Son of man, is constantly identifying with us, entering deeply into the weakness, sickness, sordidness, and death in which we are involved in order to communicate to us his strength, healing, cleansing and new life.

If the incarnation is to be understood in the light of the atonement, the atonement also must be understood in the light of the incarnation. If the Word of God assumed fallen flesh in the incarnation, then we can view the atonement as the reconciliation of *this* particular man with God, and as the redemption of *his* flesh. Within this one incarnate life we see the atonement already accomplished. As Karl Barth says: 'Jesus Christ is not what He is – very God, very man, very God-man – in order as such to do and accomplish something else which is atonement. But His being as God and man and God-man consists in the complete act of the reconciliation.'[7]

'In Him,' says Bosc, 'are reunited and unified in a single person the two beings separated by an abyss: the holy God unable to see iniquity, and man, the prisoner of sin and enslaved by corruption.'[8] In Jesus God turns to man to pardon him and call him into communion with himself, and man turns towards God and receives everything.[9] God, having laid hold of wayward human nature, 'bent it back into obedience' to himself.[10]

Here in the incarnate Lord himself is a miracle of grace. Wikenhauser suggests that Paul often wrote 'in Christ' in contexts where we should expect to find 'by Christ' because he was pointing out that Christ was the abode of God's gracious presence, the place where God willed and worked in the salvation of men.[11] Following this theme Calvin quotes Augustine: God 'made righteous this man of the seed of David, never to be unrighteous without any merit of His will preceding.'[12]

Equally in the incarnate Lord is a miracle of response to grace – a man in perfect obedience to the grace of God: in this way we have a salvation achieved by Christ as man, and by Christ as God. 'For there is now in man', says Scott Holland, 'one spot at least clean from defilement, on which the eyes of God's purity can afford to rest.' Hitherto there had been 'not one whom God could forgive. But now there is the Son of Man, in and through whom God's forgiveness can begin to work.'[13] In Jesus Christ, God's grace produced a lifelong sinlessness – a lifelong obedience to God's will that bound him to the purpose for which he had come into the world. His obedience was not simply an obedience *in* death but an obedience '*unto* death' (Phil. 2:8).

Jesus' sinless obedience was apparent in many different ways. He kept the moral law, the ten commandments. He himself was 'undefiled' (Heb. 7:26) by the vanity and sordidness of what he had entered in order to save the world. He was revolutionary where tradition was evil. He was conservative where tradition was healthy. He maintained freedom always to go his own way. But in relation to God his obedience took the form of complete self-sacrifice to the Father's will in everything. He refused to be independent in any thought or decision: 'He did nothing, said nothing, willed nothing apart from God,' says Moberly. 'He was absolutely loyal in dependence; He was absolutely without any self-reservation, any nursing of separateness of self. He was the exposition, by willing reflection, of another.'[14]

Jesus' sinlessness was the work of God's grace, but it was achieved by intense, indeed agonising effort. 'The sinlessness of Jesus was not a condition of his being as *man*, but the human act of his life.'[15] Since his sinlessness was the work of God's grace it must follow that for him to sin was impossible.[16] And yet temptation was real. There was, says Moberly, 'in his human nature, the natural machinery for, or capability of, rebelling'.[17] Jesus had to deny this 'self' – this 'pressure towards rebellion', and 'he learned obedience through the things which he suffered.' 'Disregarding his own feelings,' said Calvin, 'He subjected and yielded Himself wholly to His Father's will.' Such a subjection was achieved only 'through a stupendous act of energy or victorious moral goodness'.[18]

Jesus' obedience was geared to fulfilling a purpose he consciously understood and accepted, and felt 'sent' to fulfil. 'Jesus,' says P. T. Forsyth, 'obeyed the necessity of an actual historic and spiritual situation.' There was a 'divine must' which Israel's history was set to serve and failed. Jesus came to be the true Israel and to fulfil Israel's history.[19] He recognised himself as the one promised in all the prophesies. His obedience was not simply the obedience required of a private individual, but that of a redeemer in this historical situation. In this sense he was obedient in the fulfilment of an office. 'It is obedience – not in the general ethical sense but in the specifically Christian sense, in the sense peculiar to the Messiah.'[20]

Jesus' obedience involved his dying when and as he did, a death designed by God as a sacrifice for the sin of all mankind. His life had to lead up to this, and it was his constantly obedient life that gave value to what he offered in his death. His life could have had no redeeming value apart from his death. It was not the mere achievement of death but the unfailing obedience that was within and behind his death, that atoned for sin. His obedience in life led up to his obedience in death. All through it was his obedience that was atoning.[21]

Theologians have distinguished the 'active' obedience of Jesus from the 'passive' obedience, and have sometimes evaluated the rôle of each in effecting the atonement. There is certainly a mixture of energetic activity and total passivity in the picture of Jesus given in the Gospels. We could select texts which depict Jesus striding actively towards the cross, taking the initiative, controlling: 'I lay down my life that I might take it again.'[22] Yet we could also, by a different selection, depict Jesus as always passive in his suffering and death; striving for a great and godly success which evaded him; accepting rejection and the catastrophe that came upon him with resignation.

Pannenberg seems to suggest that the latter picture is most true to the original. He believes that the writers who later formed the Gospel tradition transposed the divine plan which was worked out in his career into his early consciousness, thus inserting predictions of his death into the story. It was this that misled Anselm to understand Jesus' death as something he had 'actually done' instead of 'something that happened to him'.[23] Brunner on the other hand saw in the aspect rejected by Pannenberg the 'genuine picture' of the historical Jesus, freshly discovered for us by the more recent criticism of the Gospels.[24]

But we have to ask whether the process of analysing texts, making selection and separation, is not bound to produce too artificial a picture. Ordinary Christians often feel most free when, before God, they feel themselves under the greatest constraint of circumstances; and they become most active when they know their activity to be determined.

In the quite unique case of Jesus, we make most sense of his redeeming mission when we allow ourselves to see both the active and passive elements in his obedient life as indivisible, exactly in the way the Gospel story presents them. As Hans W. Frei describes it: 'The enacted intention of Jesus – to obey God and enact men's good on their behalf – meshes with the external circumstances that devolved upon him.'

Frei finds in Jesus' obedience 'a co-existence of power and powerlessness in his situation and a transition from the one to the other'; and also a 'simultaneous exercise of both power and powerlessness'. He links this in a remarkable way with the words, 'He saved others, himself he cannot save.' He points out that it is Jesus' 'vicarious identification with the guilty, and at the climax of the story his identification with the helplessness of the guilty, that provide the Gospel's story of salvation. Something of his power abides and is actualised as he becomes helpless. The pattern of exchange becomes the means of salvation.'[25]

THE LIFELONG SUFFERING OF JESUS AND THE CRUCIALITY OF THE CROSS

'Atonement,' said Campbell, 'is rightly conceived as a development of the incarnation.'[26] There is certainly truth in this statement if it is interpreted in the way we have already indicated. Interpreted otherwise, it could be misleading. There was something crucial about Jesus' sufferings on the cross that cannot be reduced to simply such a 'development'.

Theologians have never failed to think about the nature and significance of Jesus' lifelong sufferings. Aquinas and Luther spoke of the great burden of his inward suffering due to his sympathy (see pp. 80–81). The seventeenth-century divines made the same observation even more emphatically. Thomas Goodwin, for example, says, 'He had a heart soft, and framed to compassion; therefore when any of his elect were sick, and brought to him, he by a feeling of pity took their griefs on him, and freed them.' Thus 'in sympathy and pity' he bore all our frailties and sicknesses.[27]

Jonathan Edwards, a century later, uses language which suggests that such lifelong suffering in Jesus has a redeeming quality. He claims that even ordinary human sympathy for others tends to 'make their case ours', 'places us in their position' and enables us to suffer 'in their stead'. Therefore 'in that great act of suffering' wherein Christ 'specially stood for them and was substitute in their stead, his love and pity fixed the idea of them in his mind as if he had really been they.'[28] He is asserting that in the make-up of Christ's sufferings on the cross, itself an important ingredient, was the same burden-bearing sympathy of his human heart reaching out to humanity, as had characterised his whole life. Here Edwards comes very close in thought to McLeod Campbell.

Though both Goodwin and Edwards insisted on the power of Christ's sympathy to enable him to take our sufferings to his heart, they also insisted that there was a further element in his sufferings – a penal element. In no way was this to be accounted for by the natural outgoing of his human soul. For Goodwin, the sufferings that came to Christ, especially during his final passion, were due to his encountering the wrath of God. The second Adam first encountered the Father's anger in the Garden of Gethsemane. And the substance of this suffering was 'the same that we in hell should have undergone'.[29] Goodwin admits that even before the crucifixion – for example, in his temptation – some of the elements that made his final suffering so unique could have burdened his life already:

From his birth all the great ordinance of God's curses were ready, charged with wrath, and bent against him, and were all in their order discharged, and let off upon him. And therefore not his suffering, but his sufferings are mentioned by Peter (1 Pet. 4:13) . . . He was crossed, ere he was crucified even through his whole life.[30]

Edwards is just as emphatic as Goodwin about the extra element that Christ had to bear in our place, especially on the cross. There he experienced the 'special fruit of the wrath of God' in that God 'let loose upon Christ the devil, who has the power of death, is God's executioner, and the roaring lion that devours the doomed in hell.'[31] Indeed, according to Edwards, Christ on the cross suffered 'that which the damned in hell do not suffer. For they do not see the hateful nature of sin. They have no idea of sin in itself.'[32]

However, in Britain by the middle of the nineteenth century the question arose acutely: need we affirm that there was anything penal in the sufferings of Christ even on the cross, that made them so unique to himself?

A division appeared among theologians. R. W. Dale affirmed that Christ's sufferings ultimately were beyond our capacity to experience and understand (see p. 91). In contrast, F. D. Maurice asserted firmly that 'Christ must not be put at a distance from us, as bearing sufferings to us inconceivable; it was our actual miseries and griefs into which he entered.'[33]

The wish to understand all Jesus' sufferings psychologically has, of course, continued, and so has the tendency to assimilate what happened on the cross to what happened during his life. W. Pannenberg, for instance, insists that Jesus' cross must be understood 'in the context of his human path', and he claims that Luther's description of the penal suffering of Jesus as affliction of conscience comes remarkably close to such an understanding.[34]

In other ways than by analysis of Jesus' sufferings has the attempt been made to minimise the uniqueness of his final passion. 'The real Gospel,' says Bushnell, 'is the Incarnate Biography itself, making its impression and making its effect as a biography – a total life with all its acts, and facts, and words, and feelings, and principles of good, grouped in the light and shade of their own supernatural unfolding.'[35] There is no special mention here of Jesus' death, for this was simply incidental to his life.

Heiko Oberman points out that in the Middle Ages Gabriel Biel insisted that Christ's passion was his continual suffering, beginning at his moment of birth, in the flight to Egypt, and in the poverty of his youth. God demanded from Jesus, above all, perseverance in righteousness under such sufferings. In contrast to Anselm, Biel regarded the cross as the incidental culmination of such a life.[36]

This line of thought finds summary in the assertion of J. M. Wilson: 'The incarnation is itself the atonement.'[37] More recently G. S. Hendry, emphasising that Jesus offered forgiveness to those he met during his life, has said:

If the incarnation be interpreted in the 'existentialist' terms of the Biblical testimony rather than in the 'essentialist' categories of Greek philosophy, if, that is to say, it be understood not merely as the assumption of our nature, but as the living of the incarnate life in personal relations with men at the human level, then we may say with truth that salvation is by the incarnation.

Accordingly, the 'uniqueness' that we find in the Gospel 'is not in the death nor in what it accomplished, but solely in the person who died.'[38]

There is, no doubt, continuity between Jesus' life and death. The one is congruous with the other. As Moberly puts it: 'The life exhibits much of the significance of the death.'[39] We have already noted that it was not his death simply in itself that gave value to his sacrifice, but the obedience in his death. His obedience did not vary from childhood on. Max Warren, repeating Athanasius' emphasis on the necessity of the life that led to the death, puts the case well:

> Jesus Christ lived the cross before he died upon it. His living was the teaching upon which the cross itself threw the light of a vast illumination. Unless we can see this, and understand that all Christ's living was a dying, we shall not plumb the depths of what is involved for us in our ministry of teaching.[40]

Sometimes the Gospel of the New Testament so emphasises the death that for a moment other things about Jesus fade into the background – he died for us! This was no incidental development, but was what his life led up to, moving always on and constrained always to find this consummation. This expressed its true meaning and purpose.

> The death [says A. M. Ramsey] is the deepest point of the Son of God's identification of Himself with men and of His entry into the stream of human life. If He is near to men in the joyful contact of His ministry in Galilee, teaching, healing and blessing, He is nearer still as He goes to the Cross. Remote from all the superficialities of life and of society Christ enters by way of the Cross into nearer and nearer contact with the grim realities of sin and creatureliness and death. For death is not merely a physical fact . . . it has a moral meaning since it marks and declares the sinfulness and fragmentariness of mankind.[41]

The incarnation would have been torn asunder if Christ had refused to drink the 'cup'. His death sealed the incarnation and made it effective. Instead of regarding his death as a part of his life, then, perhaps we are nearer the truth when, with Denney, we regard his life as part of his death.[42]

On this matter our interpretation at one point is decisive: what did Christ shrink from in Gethsemane, and what was he caught up within when he uttered his cry of dereliction? John Owen points out that this took place 'when there was no hand or instrument outwardly appearing to put him to any suffering or cruciating torment'.[43] It is as if he were suffering now solely from the hand of God himself – or at least in a region and manner quite beyond our understanding. No doubt this is why Luther and Calvin called these sufferings his descent into hell. We have to remember that even at this stage in his life the cross was not only terrifying but an enigma to the human Jesus.

Traditionally three features have been selected to mark out the uniqueness of the final experience on the cross. Each seems valid. Each of us must determine how far our thoughts are prepared to go.

Some have stressed the fact that God in some way hid his face. Pannenberg has been the most recent writer to suggest that Jesus' death had this 'special character', for he died 'not only as one condemned by the Roman state, but as one rejected by his people in the name and by the authority of his God.' Jesus' death was not simply a 'final biological fact' or a 'contradiction of human longing and destiny' but the death of a sinner rejected from God's eternal life. This, to one who, more than anyone else, had always been conscious of God's nearness, deserved, according to Pannenberg, to be called a descent into hell.[44]

Other writers on the atonement stress that in his final experience on the cross Jesus agonised as never before because he was brought into the closest encounter with human sin and guilt: he was immersed in a full vision of it all. 'Himself without sin,' says A. B. Macaulay, 'He was able, and He alone was able, to measure its awful grossness, its cancerous deep-rootedness in human nature, its insatiable malevolence, and its virulent hostility to goodness.'[45] And in this his sufferings are completely beyond us, for who of us could gauge, grasp, measure, 'the abysmal perdition of humanity'[46]?

Finally: 'The Fathers have many pretty interpreters of that great eclipse,' says Goodwin, 'but more witty than solid. The truth is, it was an evidence of God's anger.'[47]

In the death of Jesus, [writes Karl Barth], there occurs visibly, effectively and once for all the confrontation of God and man. . . . And the love of God finds in this One as the Representative of all the rest, nothing worthy of love, nothing that He can affirm or approve or praise, nothing in which He can have pleasure. . . . If man has a glory or even an exculpation and vindication to bring forward, where is God more likely to find it than at this point where he stands before the Father in the person of the Son of God Himself? Will not even the most secret good there may be in us, or at least in a few of us, be disclosed at this point? But in fact not a single argument is here adduced in our favour. The election of this One, the Representation of all by God's Son, brings a very different truth to light. For in the name of us all Jesus Christ can only produce our sins, our transgressions of the command. In His person man is shown to be a recreant and rebel, an enemy and opponent of God, whom God can meet only as such.[48]

THE MYSTERY OF THE PERSON AND THE MYSTERY OF THE WORK

Those who spent their time with Jesus when he was on earth speak about his teaching on the 'kingdom of God'. He said that one day in the future it would come and take over this present world. He also said that it had already come. They could enter it now, and experience its power in their midst. He took delight in showing them signs of its presence and power in his miracles (Luke 11:20). They saw so many they could not doubt that the world of their ordinary, daily experience had been invaded by this new realm of which Jesus spoke. Certainly it was invisible and still, indeed, 'beyond' this present world, still 'to come', but Jesus was in touch with its new transforming sources of power and life. He could bring people into healing, saving contact with it, in himself, here and now. Jesus called it the 'mystery of the kingdom of God'.[49]

The Gospel writers found the same mystery about Jesus' own person. They felt that with him they were in the presence and under the authority of one who did and said things that only God should do and say. They had often heard about the experiences of the Old Testament prophets when God came near to them, revealed himself to rebuke and encourage them. They now found that theirs was the same kind of experience. But now Jesus stood in the place of God. With him they experienced the same shattering sense of sin, amazing assurance of forgiveness, irresistible constraint to worship and devote their whole lives to him, even to death. When they saw him transfigured they experienced a theophany as vivid as any that came to Moses or Isaiah or Ezekiel. Yet always they dealt with the man, Jesus.

Their forefathers had made countless pilgrimages to the temple at Jerusalem, seeking and sometimes finding this kind of experience. They had believed it came to people only at the threshold of an eternal world. But they themselves were receiving it in the presence of Jesus! They concluded that what they had seen and heard in his presence was not a temporary alien irruption into his life: it belonged permanently and essentially to him as a person. It was always there, though often hidden. He was also the man, the Galilean, the son of Mary, the rabbi, but he 'moved at ease between two worlds', and seemed to belong to both. In fellowship with him they too seemed to find partial entrance into the kingdom of God itself.

A. E. Taylor, speaking of the experience of the early church after Pentecost, suggests that what gathered and held the early disciples around Jesus was not his moral perfection, his great teaching, but first and foremost 'the direct and immediate impression made by his whole personality of the presence in him of something "numinous" not to be understood in terms of the categories of ordinary human life; and secondly, the confirmation of this impression by the transcendent events of the resurrection and Pentecost.'[50]

We could collect many testimonies from the later history of the church of how the sense of the 'numinous' about Jesus continued to be experienced in very much the same way as it was by the apostles. Calvin describes what he himself must often have felt about Jesus: 'Christ stretches forth His hand that He may lead us to heaven.'[51] A century later, Bossuet says more dramatically and fully:

> We must realise the fact once-for-all, that the life of the greatest in God's Kingdom does not move in the sober light of every day, but that a large part of it lies in regions to us mysterious and unfamiliar. . . . When a flash from this innermost life touches our souls, when its depths are stirred and rise up with volcanic force, we stand amazed, and begin dimly to conceive the terribly inward greatness of such a soul-life. So it was . . . with Jesus.[52]

Without doubt today within the fellowship of the church, as we hear of him, read his word, study him, come to him with faith, as he offers us the fellowship of his inner life, we too find ourselves on the same threshold as these early Christians, facing the same new world, the kingdom of God, and gaining an entrance and foothold within it. H. R. Mackintosh, describing the impression made upon us by reading about his sinless life, 'outstripping the power of the imagination, and almost of belief', writes: 'Here is a casement opening on a diviner world.'[53]

This sense of an extraordinary presence in Jesus can be paralleled in our account of how the first disciples viewed the cross afterwards. No doubt at first Jesus' death appeared to them as accidental. But it could not have been long before they began to understand the death in terms of a sacrificial death offered to God for sin, like one of their Old Testament sacrifices. They began to look on it as the great final sacrifice to which all the others pointed.

To people who had met and worshipped God through the Old Testament sacrifices there was mystery in what took place through the ritual, and the form of service was designed to enhance its transcendental nature. Karl Heim asks us to imagine the experience of the waiting congregation of Israel on the Day of Atonement. 'They could only watch the High Priest disappear before their eyes into the Holy of Holies, there, in the presence of God, to accomplish the atonement.' What most mattered happened beyond their ken.[54] Von Rad, explaining their approach to the meaning and efficacy of their sacrifices, says that 'However deep our understanding can probe there comes an absolute limit beyond which no further explanation is possible . . . and it is precisely this most important aspect of the sacrifice which takes place beyond this limit', i.e., in a 'sphere lying outside of man and his spirituality'.[55]

The members of the early church, now seeing the cross as the place where Jesus offered himself as a sacrifice, felt compelled to invest his offering there with the same transcendent significance as belonged to the Old Testament sacrifices. They saw him as crucified between earth and heaven. His cries in Gethsemane and on the cross became to them the utterances of one engaged in a struggle and agony in the depths of an invisible world.[56] 'The great mass of Christ's work,' wrote P. T. Forsyth, 'was like a stable iceberg. It was hidden. It was His dealing with God, not man. The great thing was done with God. It was independent of our knowledge of it. The most ever done for us was done behind our backs. Only it was we who had turned our backs.'[57]

We have been discussing singly the mystery of the person and the mystery of the work. They were of course closely related within the developing thought of the church. Great affirmations came about his person, such as 'in him dwelt all the fullness of the Godhead in bodily form', and finally the church expressed its views in the statements of Nicaea and Chalcedon. Equal affirmations were made about his work. They had visions of Jesus reconciling all things in heaven and earth to God, opening up a new way into the holiest of all, and breaking the power of every law and evil force that could hold mankind in captivity.

The order of our discussion here is not meant to suggest that their conviction about the person of Christ developed before their conviction about the atonement. More probably it happened the other way round. 'The doctrine of the incarnation grew upon the church out of its experience of the atonement. The church was forced on the deity of Christ to account for its redeemed existence in Christ,' says P. T. Forsyth, adding wisely, 'We can experience the redemption as we cannot experience the incarnation.'[58] Yet we assert that only after the church attained and expressed its full christological conviction was an adequate basis provided for understanding the atonement. In this sense we agree with Pannenberg, 'Soteriology must follow from Christology, not vice versa. Otherwise faith in salvation loses any foundation.'[59]

The orthodox doctrine of the person of Christ, taken by itself, has often been called abstract and unrelated to life. Nevertheless it has proved an indispensable key to fuller meaning of the atonement. 'Here you see how necessary it is to believe and confess the doctrine of the divinity of Christ,' writes Luther. 'When Arius denied this, it was necessary also for him to deny the doctrine of redemption. For to conquer the sin of the world, death, the curse, and the wrath of God in Himself – this is the work not of any creature but of divine power.'[60]

It is illuminating to see how in the history of the doctrine emphasis on different aspects of the person of Christ brought out different aspects of his redeeming work.

During the patristic age the work of the atonement was seen as the work of God. God himself was regarded as entering our plight and conflict, and as acting, suffering, overcoming in and through the man Jesus. God was 'the effective agent', initiating and authorising every-thing, as Aulén puts it, 'from beginning to end'.[61] The human nature is, in this view, simply an instrument in the divine hand. But with Anselm came a theory of the atonement in which the man Jesus was regarded as himself the agent, working out salvation at man's side, acting towards God and even on God, though God himself certainly had a prior initiative, and the divinity gave value to the work of the humanity.

In Luther and Calvin the switch of emphasis is repeated. Luther stresses the divine work in the atonement.[62] At times he gives the impression that for him the humanity is instrumental. Calvin corrects the balance, and insists that the man Christ Jesus is not a 'mere instrument' in the hands of God but that we ought to seek 'the matter of our salvation' in him.[63]

We must try to preserve what is valuable in both approaches to understanding the atonement. Undoubtedly the initiative and priority lay with God himself. Even those theories which picture Jesus as acting and suffering so that he prevailed over God include a prior covenant initiated by God in which Jesus was appointed to fulfil such a rôle. Gustav Aulén rightly depreciates all thought of an atonement being 'interrupted by an offering made to God from man's side'.[64] But under the grace of God the atonement was also the achievement of the man Christ Jesus. He was elected, conceived and born for this purpose.

The conditions of his life, his personal, social and political battles, and his temptations, are familiar to all of us, especially the poor and deprived. Much of his suffering is ours too. But within this life he perfectly fulfilled his unique vocation of atoning suffering and death. In doing this his divinity gave real value, depth and effectiveness to his human work before God, so that we can speak of him as influencing God and as prevailing with God. It is *God* as man who achieves all this in the place of all of us, but it is God actually *as man* who does it. And God in inspiring and sanctifying the man Jesus for the work allows him human freedom and human initiative with such generous grace that we can think of the work as accomplished by man. And this work is not separate and supplementary to the atonement. It is an essential though distinct aspect of the one work.

Seen geared to the atonement, orthodox Christology loses entirely its 'metaphysical' or its 'mythological' character. It becomes closely related to life because it explains Christ as he was in what he did. It is difficult to see how any other view of the person of Christ can provide a framework for a view of the atonement capable of illuminating with such fullness and detail the whole New Testament picture of his work. Viewed in this light the orthodox Christology becomes a very practical doctrine, for the force and vigour of the Christian life we live depends upon the view of the redemption from which it springs.

8 The heart of the atonement

THE MEETING PLACE BETWEEN GOD AND MAN

In many of their temple ceremonies of worship, the people of Israel aimed to offer a fitting tribute to the exalted Lord of heaven and earth – the Redeemer of the nation. But at their religious feasts when they gathered from all over the holy land to pay their tribute and vows, they had other aims also. At the heart of their worship, at the altar, they sought a communion, a word, a conversation as intimate and individual as possible between the redeeming one and the soul. The Psalms tell us that at all the great feasts and occasions they expected God to 'appear', and 'show his face'. The Psalms are full of expressions of repentance, hope and thanksgiving of the community, but they also contain longings, confessions and thanksgivings that are intimately personal.

Their whole temple liturgy shows us why the people went to Jerusalem. Life was empty and dead without God. Like the bride in the Song of Solomon they yearned to meet him again – and they did regularly at the altar of sacrifice. Indeed, God had instituted the cult because he *was* their bridegroom. He too longed to meet them – in spite of their unfaithfulness. The sacrifices were there to show his forgiveness, and to reaffirm his holiness in his forgiving. The ark was the sign of his presence, and to them it meant what the Lord's Supper means to us at a communion service. There he came to inspire their love and fear of him, to receive their worship and renewed surrender.

When Christ died the veil of the temple was torn in two from top to bottom (Matt. 27:51), because temple, altar and sacrifice were all now replaced. The presence Israel had longed for, feared and enjoyed at the altar is now given in a better way. The cross is our meeting place with God. Here we are at the heart of what the atonement means:

Is not the Cross the meeting point between man and man, between man and God? Is not this meeting point what men in all times and places, have been seeking for? Did any find it till God declared it? And are we not bringing our understanding to the foot of this Cross, when we solemnly adjure all schemes and statements, however sanctioned by the arguments of the divines, however plausible as implements of declamation, which prevent us from believing and proclaiming that in it all the wisdom and truth and glory of God are manifested to the creature; that in it man is presented as a holy and acceptable sacrifice to the creator?[1]

The Bible, Israel's history and the cross itself teach us to find wrath as well as love expressed within the encounter between the holy God and sinners. Too readily we think of God's wrath as reserved only for those abandoned by his love to utter destruction, or as being mixed up with ill-will and vindictiveness. We forget that in the Old Testament God's wrath is there where he seeks fellowship with us. It is active where his love is active – to destroy the evil, confusion and darkness that prevent the activity and reception of his love, and to annihilate the will that unrepentingly opposes his love. As Stephen Neil puts it: 'The alternative to wrath is neutrality – neutrality to the conflict of the world . . . It is only the doctrine of the wrath of God, of his irreconcilable hostility to all evil, which makes life tolerable in such a world as ours.'[2] 'If God does not meet us in His jealous zeal and wrath,' writes Karl Barth, 'exactly as He meets Israel according to the witness of the Old Testament, exactly as He meets us later in the crucifixion of His own Son – then He does not meet us at all.'[3]

Thus at the cross, as part of God's longing for communion with his people we find full and free expression of his holy wrath against sin. Again we quote F. D. Maurice:

Since nowhere is the contrast between infinite love and infinite evil brought before us as it is there [i.e. in the cross], we have the fullest right to affirm that the Cross exhibits the wrath of God against sin, and the endurance of that wrath by the well-beloved Son. For wrath against that which is unlovely is not the counteracting force to love, but the attribute of it. Without it love would be a name, and not a reality.[4]

It is in the light of this unique meeting at the cross in our name with the holy love of God, that we are to understand Jesus' struggle in Gethsemane and the 'Amen' with which he accepted the cup he had to drink.

McLeod Campbell at this point regarded him as making a perfect confession of our sins to the Father. Moberly interpreted the situation as revealing Christ's experience and acceptance of the perfect sin-consciousness of true penitence, as giving, in obedience to God, the true offering of a contrite heart.[5]

P. T. Forsyth takes an important step forward in illuminating the matter. He points out that the great work of Christ was not so much to confess human sin, 'but to confess something greater, namely God's holiness in His judgment upon sin. His confession, indeed, was made not in so many words, but in a far more mighty way, by act and deed of life and death. . . . He confessed God's holiness in reacting mortally against human sin, in cursing human sin, in judging it to its very death.'[6] Jesus, says Forsyth again, 'felt sin with God, and sin's judgment with men.'[7]

In Christ's journey to God, and his meeting with both love and wrath, we have to see ourselves already included; our reconciliation with God already accomplished. We have to remember the New Testament teaching that the life, death, and resurrection of Jesus are events that involve all mankind.

> The incarnate Son of God existed, so to speak, in two capacities – in his own person and as the representative of the new humanity. Every act he wrought was performed on behalf of the new humanity which he bore in his body. That is why he is called the second Adam or the last Adam (1 Cor. 15:45). Like Christ himself, the first Adam had been both an individual and the representative of the whole human race. He too bore the whole human race in himself.[8]

In Christ God has, as it were, incorporated into himself not simply an individual person, but all human nature, indeed all mankind. We have been included in him in this way so that we can now allow ourselves to become involved in what he has done – in his meeting with God, his faithful response to God, his acknowledgement of our human sin and God's righteous condemnation. We must allow ourselves to be drawn as far as possible into what Christ encountered for us. Though he died to shelter us from the full bitterness of the curse and wrath of God, this does not mean that we are to remain sheltered from God himself. He died, says Peter, 'that he might *bring* us to God'.

THE CROSS AND THE HEART OF GOD

My dogmatics teacher H. R. Mackintosh paused in one of his lectures to say, in such a way that we were uncertain of his seriousness (though we suspected it), 'Remember, gentlemen, the cross was a quite new experience for God himself.' I puzzled over this and shortly after took down a note, with approval, from Canon Quick's book that 'Jesus did not suffer vicariously for God.'[9] Recently I have put beside it a quotation from Paul Althaus, 'Jesus died for God before he died for us.' This is cited in Moltmann's book *The Crucified God*, in a section where he refers to 'new converging trends of theological thought' which 'attempt to understand God's being from the death of Jesus and compel us to ask "What did the cross of Jesus mean for God himself?" ' He refers to Karl Rahner's inquiries as to what extent God himself is 'affected by' the fate of Jesus on the cross, and to Karl Barth's almost 'theopaschite' references to God's suffering and being involved in the cross of his Son.[10]

Undoubtedly the cross tells about the being and heart of God as well as about his activity. 'God is revealed *in it*,' insists McLeod Campbell, 'and not merely *in connexion with it*.'[11] He finds God's righteousness and love *in* the suffering itself.

Luther, more than any other theologian, underlines this aspect of the revelation given in the cross. In his teaching, as Paul Althaus remarks, 'God in Christ deals . . . with himself, in himself, and in an inner trinitarian relationship.'[12] In this inward tension divine love 'prevails over the wrath, the blessing overcomes the curse by way of divine self oblation and sacrifice'.[13] Out of this inner tension there arises the strange 'contrariety', as Barth calls it, in the conduct of God towards his own people – a sign of his 'anger and struggle against sin'.[14] All this, Aulén asserts, 'shows how much the atonement costs God'.[15] The decision to forgive, and the outgoing forgiveness, involved God in what Karl Heim calls an 'innermost sacrifice': 'He whose wrath we have deserved tears something from his own heart and gives it for our sakes.'[16] It is an entirely superficial view, even in human life, to regard forgiveness as in any way simple or easy.[17]

It has been popularly held that the costly suffering in God's heart, of which the cross gives us some reflection, is eternal. Bushnell has given vivid expression to this idea:

There is a cross in God before the wood is seen upon Calvary; hid in God's own virtue itself, struggling on heavily in burdened feeling through all the previous ages, and struggling as heavily now even in the throne of the worlds. This, too, exactly, is the cross that our Christ crucified reveals and sets before us.[18]

C. A. Dinsmore also enlarges on this: 'As the flash of the volcano discloses for a few hours the elemental forces at earth's centre, so the light of Calvary was the bursting forth through historical conditions of the very nature of the everlasting.'[19]

All this is so stated as to suggest that the atonement takes place in eternity rather than in time. Donald Baillie, who has been the most vigorous recent upholder of this view, asserts that the cross 'is the point in human history where we find the actual outcropping of the divine atonement'[20]: God's sin-bearing was incarnate in Jesus' passion, but Calvary itself has made no real difference to God, for his sin-bearing now continues all the time.[21] To support this Baillie points to the wounds borne in the hands of the risen Lord, and to Paul's vision on the Damascus road in which Jesus speaks as one who is still persecuted. Baillie seems to link up Christ's heavenly intercession with this continuous heavenly sin burden, and quotes with approval a statement of Gore that Christ's propitiation and intercession are identical.[22] Baillie points out that such a view was prevalent in the thought of the Greek Orthodox Church.

However strong its appeal may be to many today, such a view lends a meaning to the cross which contradicts the form of the cross itself. We have clear witness that the sufferings of Christ were finished before he rose again and ascended to heaven. What happened in time, at the heart of revelation, has no deception about it. Jesus took his humanity to heaven, his memory, and his compassionate love. As the Scottish paraphrase puts it:

> He still remembers in the skies
> His tears and agonies and cries.

But he did not take his agony, and the wounds he wore were the signs of who he was and of what he had done. The 'lamb slain in the midst of the throne' is not crying out in deathly agony. John Donne in one of his sermons asks us to think of how the angels behold the risen Christ 'sate down in glory at the right hand of his Father, all sweat wyp'd from his browes, all teares from his eyes: all his stripes healed, all his blood staunch'd, all his woundes shut up, and all His beauty returned there.'[23]

9 The framework of the atonement

LOVE ENCLOSED IN LAW

Our view of the atonement is that Christ died to 'bring us to God', and in the two previous sections we have discussed what we see and find as God comes to meet us in Christ. We could indeed call this the 'heart of the atonement'. But the atonement is bigger than its heart, and some form of the doctrine of penal substitution is required to provide the framework of the heart. Christ, says Peter, 'died *the righteous for the unrighteous*, that he might lead us to God.'

Often given a crude expression, this doctrine has been subjected to much harsher criticism than it has deserved. Its faults are obvious. It draws our attention from the real battle between God and man, God and evil, God and his Son, to a 'transaction in a civil court in which the judge and the accused come to an understanding according to fixed rules of procedure'.[1] It puts abstract justice rather than God on the throne of the universe. It suggests that Christ's righteousness can really be transferred to us and our guilt transferred to him, in an external way. It suggests that sin is of such an essence that its punishment can be measured quantitatively and its equivalent executed on a substitute.

But we are justified in seeing God's work in the atonement as having to do with the upholding and manifestation of his law. The God who wills and presides at the cross has in it 'magnified the law and made it honourable'. The cross itself proclaims God's 'inflexible regard for the law', and 'his unfailing demand for its fulfilment'.[2] God's law and God's love are very close to each other all through the biblical story. At Sinai the law was given to those he had first loved so much as to redeem from bondage (Gal. 3:17 ff). The law, written on tablets, was enclosed within the ark in the tabernacle: thus at Sinai we see the law at the centre, enclosed in love. But at Calvary we see love at the centre, yet enclosed in law.[3]

God's justice is always exalted in the Old Testament as an aspect of his goodness and saving love. The prophet Isaiah exalts him as 'a just God and (therefore) a Saviour', and the psalmists seek deliverance from their sin and distress by his 'righteousness' as well as by his love and omnipotence.[4] In redeeming us God, as ruler and judge of the universe, seeks to give us a liberty that is much more than a new inner confidence in, or life of sonship before, him.

McLeod Campbell rejected the penal theory because it resulted in 'the substitution of a legal standing for a filial standing as the gift of God in Jesus Christ'.[5] But it is to God's glory that he knows our need and gives us both, instead of substituting the one for the other. 'The relationship of father and child,' says Denney, 'are undoubtedly more adequate to the truth than those of judge and criminal . . . but so far as our experience of them goes, they are not equal to it.'[6] Psalm 103, which stresses so much God's forgiving love, his mercy and fatherliness, also speaks of his *crowning* us with lovingkindness, and working 'vindication and justice' for us in our oppression.

It is true that we must not regard God as being enclosed in an 'iron framework' of law, binding him to 'vindicate his honour', dictating what he must do or not do.[7] We must affirm God's freedom. Even John Owen insisted that it was false to assert that God could not have mercy unless satisfaction was made by his Son. Scripture, he said, affirms no such thing. Other ways of saving, as Augustine says, were open to God.[8] We can, however, regard justice as the law of God's being, and indeed of his love. It is grounded in the nature of God himself. God could not ignore sin because he cannot ignore his own holiness. His way in the atonement is an expression of himself. We can therefore speak of a necessity for the atonement, but it is a necessity that arises from within God himself, and is such that it is hidden from us until we find God revealed, and this necessity expressed, in the atonement.

The law which we relate to God's activity in the atonement is not prior to love, nor is love bound by it. But something of God is reflected in it, and it was made an essential part of human life when God created man out of his love and in order to reflect his image. In human life love is always expressed and enjoyed in its healthiest and most stable form when it is enclosed within a sworn, binding covenant with moral obligations to faithfulness. In this way God seeks to preserve love and give human life the stability, order and meaning in which alone love can find its highest expression.[9]

We believe that in this connection we cannot disregard the penal aspect of Christ's sufferings on the cross. We have already suggested that this was the aspect that put his sufferings beyond our understanding or our powers of experience. According to the New Testament Jesus tasted death in its full horror, death with the 'sting of sin' fully active within it. It is precisely such a death that forms the 'wages of sin', and we are spared precisely this penalty because he took it all, and in taking it he took it away. For us he entered into the region of the penalty and curse of sin. But where he went we cannot follow.

In our view it is in accord with the New Testament to speak, as Anselm did, of some kind of 'satisfaction' rendered to God from the side of man. Brunner suggests that Anselm may have chosen the word 'satisfaction' because it holds the balance between the ideas of penalty and sacrifice.[10] Yet in our use of such a term we have to avoid implying that it was harshly executed by God, and we have to exclude all idea of revenge or self-gratification on God's part. We have a perfect expression of the kind of satisfaction God had in Christ: at his baptism the voice came: 'This is my beloved Son, in whom I am well pleased.'

It is often suggested that in retaining the idea that Christ's sufferings are penal we need not think of them as retributive. Christ's sufferings, it is argued, are 'penal' only in the sense that he was punished as an example to deter others from sinning and so to help God to maintain the moral order of the universe. Such a view does not reflect truly the witness of the New Testament. Christ, in the very declaration he made of God's righteousness on the cross, bore our sins in his own person. To proclaim the cross as a mere deterrent without relation to what is to be done about each and all of our own sins cannot possibly bring the comfort and liberty to the human conscience that the New Testament preaching conveys.[11]

The traditional theory of penal substitution becomes most difficult to defend when it asserts that Christ received a punishment equivalent to that which we should have borne. 'Does it mean,' asks Forsyth, 'that in the hour of his death Christ suffered, compressed into one brief moment, all the pains of hell that the human race deserved?'[12] Some have thought so, and have said so decisively. Shedd affirmed that the satisfaction must be 'mathematically equivalent to the whole punishment due in the case of every sinner and of every sin'. Even Anselm spoke of God as 'demanding proportionate satisfaction'.[13] Here we have to ask whether Peter, when he said 'He bore our sins', really had their exact weight in mind, or whether Paul, when he said 'that he might be righteous', really meant us to think of an exact amount (1 Pet. 2:24; Rom. 3:26).

There is no doubt that the human conscience in its awakened search for pardon, when trying to make amends, often thinks in terms of an offering or punishment equivalent to the wrong deemed to be done. As Brunner says, 'The idea of an equivalent which lies behind the idea of sacrifice would not have exercised such an immense influence, it would not have been so widespread and tenacious all through the course of history, were it not for the fact that behind it lies a deep truth.'[14]

Justice means justice! God himself in Israel's life encouraged the idea of costly sacrifice to make amends for serious sin. But does not the sacrificial system in Israel suggest that what God both gives and demands is not so much an exact equivalent but an adequate equivalent? And are we not meant to accept as adequate what he himself gives us as such?

Indeed we have to accept gratefully the fact that the sacrifice of Christ is in God's sight far more than an equivalent for what sin has done. We must remind ourselves of Aquinas' thought of a superabundant satisfaction (see p. 76). Surely it is the *way* Jesus lived and the way he suffered that gives infinite value to his death in the eyes of God, and not the intensity of the pains he bore. In this sense we can affirm, 'precious in the sight of the Lord is the death of his saints' (Psa. 116:15). To what purpose, then, is spiritual and moral arithmetic in trying to probe what satisfies God in the matter of sacrifice and penalty for sin? And do not the demands of God's love somewhat alter, even magnify, the demands of his justice? 'Measured suffering,' says A. B. Bruce, 'especially when it is endured by so august a personage, might satisfy divine justice, but it could not satisfy divine love.'[15]

In the light of what Christ has offered and borne on Calvary, no cloud will be cast on God's righteousness should he never cease to forgive us, however great the final count of our sins might prove to be. As A. Scott Lidgett says:

> The incarnate and crucified Son of God gave, through all the experiences active and passive of His redemptive ministry, but especially through his death, the full revelation of the mind of God towards sin, His abhorrence of it, the sorrow which it causes Him, the seriousness of His abiding displeasure against it. The holy hatred of sin manifested by Christ in His Passion is God's, and the satisfaction which He demands, provides and accepts, meets the first condition of true satisfaction – that it should place in clear light and should vindicate the mind of Him to whom it is offered.[16]

OUR SUBSTITUTE AND REPRESENTATIVE

Many statements of the penal doctrine give a picture of Christ brought before God the judge as the one man innocent of all transgression. The sin of mankind is imputed to him; he takes the place of the guilty under their condemnation and sentence, so that they can go free while he is executed in their stead.

Such a picture attempts to do justice to the New Testament texts which regard Christ as undergoing our penalty, and also to the affirmations that he suffered not simply 'on our behalf' but 'in our place' and 'in our stead'.

Some writers prefer to think of Jesus standing before God as our representative rather than as a substitute, for, they point out, a representative can act with authority on behalf of, and even in the place of others. He can in many respects substitute for the community he represents. Yet the word 'representative' fails to indicated the essential difference between us and Jesus that characterises what he did. Used of Christ and interpreted with its full meaning, it would imply that he was our appointee, chosen by us as one like ourselves, deriving his authority from us, supposed to act on our instructions. The word 'substitute' is preferable. It safeguards the fact that he was given to us and for us by God and that he stood in a place where none of us can stand, went where none of us could have gone, bore in our stead what none of us could have borne.[17]

The difficulties of thinking of Jesus as our substitute are lessened if we sever its legal connection. The image of a legal imputation to Christ of our sins and guilt by a decree of God is unhelpful: rather, we must think in terms of an 'exchange' that Jesus was able to make with us within the union he was involved in in the incarnation. Throughout his incarnate life he increasingly involved himself with our evil and its consequences, in such a way that, always resisting, always hating it, he nevertheless took its burden and guilt entirely on himself.

The New Testament writers thought of Christ as making an exchange for us, and this view was current in the earliest days of the church. It came to prominence again at the Reformation (see pp. 78–81). Today it can be given effective and clear expression in the context of substitution. 'Here in Christ,' writes Heinrich Vogel, 'is a substitution or an exchange, full of wonder and comfort. Christ experienced our death and entered hell; we experience his life and enter his blessed state. Just as he takes for his own everything that is ours, including our guilt and our death, so that all that is his, his holiness and his eternal life become ours.'[18]

We must grasp two quite distinct, almost opposite, aspects of Jesus' work if we are to understand as fully as we can the doctrine of substitution. When he was on earth Jesus made people feel that he was one with them. They felt that he belonged to them more than any other individual had ever done or could ever do. And he made them feel that they belonged to him. This impression has been felt by Christians of every generation.

The church tried to explain this when it was formulating its doctrine of the person of Christ. It affirmed that when the *Logos* became incarnate he became one with all of us, not simply by assuming an isolated example of the human race to himself but, as we have pointed out,[19] by assuming our common nature. This uniqueness in the humanity of Jesus seals the bond with each member of the race. We are represented in him as in no other human being. This helps us to see how he can stand before God to act in our name.

But, quite paradoxically, people in his day were drawn to Jesus not because they felt he was *one* with them, but because they felt that he was so *different* from them. He was holy, apart, undefiled, quite unlike anybody else! Had he been merely the same as they, how could he have done for them what no other could do, and so brought them to salvation? He can substitute for humanity, therefore, not only because he represents humanity, but also because he is thus unique, and stands apart from others with his own name, his individual characteristics, his own secrets and sorrows. While the church recognised that his human nature was 'impersonal' in the sense that it was our common human nature assumed by the *Logos*, it also had to recognise that in important respects he was distinctly individual too!

He atones for us, then, both in his community with us and in his apartness from us, i.e., as our representative *and* substitute.

If we think of Christ as being simply a sinless individual, outstanding and distinct from us all, and of the rest of us as a great collection of sinful individuals each characterised by our solitary responsibility rather than by our collective, inherited sin, then those who react against the idea of transferred guilt or punishment are correct. It is 'morally and psychologically inconceivable'. But such a picture is not true either of humanity or of Christ himself. 'None of us lives to himself and none of us dies to himself' (Rom. 14:7). 'We do participate in the good and evil of another's acts,' says James Orr. 'The penalties of sin are rarely confined to the individual evil-doer. They overflow to all connected with him – descend to posterity. The innocent has to bear the load and shame of them, and often voluntarily assumes them.'[20]

All this is heightened between Christ our 'representative' and ourselves as he takes upon himself, under the grace of God, our sins and guilt. But in his apartness from us, his unique personal life, he received from God all the gifts and blessings that humanity needs and completely lacks. They are given to him that they might become ours through him. His apartness enables him to stand alone before God, even though he does it in our name, and to meet on our behalf the wrath we could not face, the punishment we could not bear, and the enemy we could not overcome. For 'he alone,' says Athanasius, 'being Word of the Father and above all, was in consequence both able to recreate all, and worthy to suffer on behalf of all and to be an ambassador for all with the Father.'[21]

CHRISTUS VICTOR

The aspect of the atonement into which we now enter can mean very little to us if we insist that there is no such thing in the world as a demonic power or a personal devil. Jesus often spoke of himself as 'casting out demons' and he attacked certain illnesses assuming that they were directly due to demon possession. If he had confined his references to demonic powers to such medical cases it would be easier for us to accept the suggestion that by using such 'mythical' conceptions he was making concessions to the ignorance of his day, and was speaking about his cures in the only way the people around him could understand.

But Jesus did not confine himself to such references. As we have already seen, he interpreted the cross as a conflict with the evil one. Satan was to him, without any possibility of pretence on his part, the dreadful enemy of all human life and goodness, challenging him, if he would save mankind, to a desperate output of all his strength, vigilance, patience and courage, if he was to have any hope of winning the battle.

The whole shape of the atonement as designed and planned by God compels us to regard evil as a personal force, sinister and powerful in its workings, ruthless in its destructive will, so titanic in its power that it could aim at robbing God of his throne. Dora Greenwell quotes de Maistre as saying, 'We do not see the Duchy of Lucca invade France, nor Genoa declare war on England.'[22] Nor do we see a great empire mobilise all its forces and resources into repelling a small or imaginary invasion by a tiny principality which has no effective ally. The way God met evil in Christ is itself proof of the strange immensity of its power.

Evil was overcome by Jesus. Evil is in retreat. But it was overcome in such a way that we too must still 'watch and pray' against it with the same vigilance as Jesus showed. The cross proves that the victory was his, and also ours. But his agony shows that we can never take any such victory as cheap and easily won, even over an enemy now all the more desperate because its final doom is sealed.

The early church for centuries gave prominence in its preaching to the proclamation of the atonement as the victory of Christ over the powers of evil. Though this aspect was ignored by Anselm it was not by Aquinas. It was strongly emphasised by Luther; and was given its due place by Calvin. In all the Puritan divines we find it fully expounded as an essential aspect of Christ's atoning work, sometimes alongside, though often after, their exposition of the penal substitution theory. John Owen remarked: 'As the judge was to be satisfied so the jailer was to be conquered.' Christ, in bringing us to God as his brothers, not only deals with the problems of our past debts and legal status, but also ensures that we are free to follow as he leads.

It may be significant that in this century little attention was given to this aspect of the atonement until after the first world war. P. T. Forsyth then wrote:

It is not from our moral lapses nor from our individual taint that we are delivered, but from world sin, sin in dominion, sin solidary if not hereditary, yea from sin which integrates us into a Satanic Kingdom. An event like the war at least aids God's purpose in this that it shocks and rouses us into some due sense of what evil is, and what a Saviour's task with it is.[23]

In 1924 there appeared an influential work called *Christus Victor*, by Gustaf Aulén, asserting that what he called the 'classic' doctrine of the atonement, including the ransom theory which prevailed in the early church for the first 900 years (i.e., before Anselm), was very close to that of the New Testament. In subsequent centuries it became sadly neglected: it must be recovered and restated. He firmly believed that the views of Anselm and Abelard belonged to the past, that the humanistic outlook which prevailed in his day was going to disappear and that the mind of the modern man was ready for a revival of the primitive theory. He believed it could be restated so as to absorb within its sweep the legal and other analogies used in the New Testament. Aulén himself, however, did not attempt such restatement, and the accuracy of some of his central statements can be challenged.[24]

Karl Heim's exposition of the atonement, *Jesus, the World Perfector*, makes this *Christus Victor* aspect central, and we can give no better guidance for understanding this view than to summarise his arguments. Heim clearly states what he sees in the background of the New Testament passion narratives:

The issue of the work of reconciliation is not merely a settlement between God and the obedient individual. Something far more difficult and terrible is at stake, *viz.* the overcoming of the diabolical power, the mortal enemy to God which becomes visible as the sinister background behind every deceit and every attack of rage. It is a good thing that we do not look down into the abyss into which we fall at every sin (p. 72).

The world has been invaded by the satanic power which hates God and is bent on dethroning him, and through our fall into sin we have allied ourselves with this. We ourselves have become possessed, even though we are unaware of it, by a spirit of hatred which defies God, and is much greater and more virulent than any malice that could have originated within our natural selves. 'Every lie in which we get entangled, every unclean desire by which we allow ourselves to get intoxicated, is surely a single spark of a volcanic eruption which aims at the destruction of God's creation.' In sin we attack God's honour and aim a deadly blow, if we can, at his innermost being (pp. 60, 94).

It is to eradicate satanic hatred within us that the apostle appeals to us to become 'reconciled to God' (p. 59). But no such reconciliation can take place without our being delivered from the power of the evil one who holds us down in our satanic alliance with him. Our reconciliation is entirely dependent on our redemption, and is accomplished when satanic power is overcome within us. Moreover, to enjoy such redemption from satanic power is to be saved from the wrath of God. Since sin is of satanic origin and inspired by satanic virulence, God can do no other but meet it with his will for its utter destruction. Heim quotes Althaus: 'Scripture . . . holds the opinion that every single sin is so terrible in God's world that God cannot answer it by anything other than his wrath' (p. 89).

The unredeemed man is caught within this world between the wrath of satan who still has power to dominate individual souls and work havoc in communities, and the wrath of God.

Here then is a clue to an important aspect of Christ's passion, and a hint of how we can think of him as bearing our sins. Christ is the mediator who places himself between the two conflicting powers. On the one hand he is on God's side. Therefore he exposes himself to the world's whole hatred of God, and the satanic powers of the world seek to limit his influence, to rob him of His godhead and dishonour him. On the other hand he is on the side of the fallen human race, whose fate he has taken on Himself: 'the destroying judgment of God's wrath' which is directed against the whole human race (pp. 96–7).

In Heim's view evil is destroyed through being drawn by Christ into a conflict which it cannot really in the end win; a conflict in which it oversteps itself and in which it is led on to express fully all it really is. It destroys itself in its self-expression. Where the Fathers of the early church viewed Jesus as a bait to draw the devil from man, Jesus in this theory, as Nathaniel Micklem points out, rather acts like a magnet. But the analogy is very similar.[25]

Again on this matter P. T. Forsyth makes a profound and helpful observation:

'Pain,' says a fine literary critic speaking of lyric art, 'cannot be conquered till it is expressed.' This is still more true of evil. Sin could not be conquered till it was expressed. And that was what Christ did in God and God in Christ. He brought evil to a moral head and dealt with it as a unity. He forced a final crisis of the universal conscience to decide it for good. He forced battle unto victory once for all for the race and for eternity.[26]

Heim finds that this theory helps us to face some of the problems which arise out of the penal substitution theory. He admits that there is an element of truth in the view that Christ took on himself the sum total of all the punishments in hell that we deserved, and also in the view that in these terrible hours he experienced the pains of a bad conscience. But such truths have been too closely bound up with the 'fantastic thought' of an incalculable number of isolated transgressions. We can better express what these assertions mean if we say that Christ was, in his final agony, fighting the unified satanic will present in us all (p. 97).

Heim also finds in the theory a satisfactory solution to the problems surrounding the idea of Christ as our 'substitute'. He feels strongly that though each of us can act vicariously for another in doing work for each other, in paying debts, in fighting battles, such a thing as guilt, e.g. in the case of perjury, falsehood or adultery, cannot be transferred. The doctrine which maintains such transference he deems immoral. But in the case of Christ's intervention for our sake, what is most at issue is a battle in which we ourselves could not possibly take part, for we too were enemies of the cause for which we would have had to fight! There is indeed only *one* who can step in where no other can stand and do battle (pp. 114–5). But having fought and won the battle in his isolation Christ now seeks to draw us into a new repentant, watchful action, for which he has set us free – 'an eternal motion within us' – though we must not include, within the vicarious work of Christ, this effect which his atonement has within us (pp. 116–7).

Heim points out that it was on Christ's sinlessness and his perfect obedience in the face of his temptations that the success of the atonement entirely depended. He had to enter into the battle pure. This is why in John's Gospel he constantly affirmed his own sinlessness in preparation for the final conflict (pp. 76–7, 82, 101–2). In this way the whole obedient life of Christ is effectively integrated with his death to become a meaningful unity.

On this view the cross is a decisive turning point in the history of mankind. It has brought about a crucial change in the relationship between God and mankind. The power of the devil though broken has not been destroyed entirely, for the final destruction of everything that spoils human life and holds the physical world in bondage has yet to come. But nothing can now interfere with the reconciliation of the individual soul with God. We await our redemption but we have our reconciliation here and now, complete (p. 180. cf. Rom. 5:11).

Heim's statement of the atonement appeals in a world in which people are deeply perplexed over the mysteries of death, moral evil, and human suffering. Many people today feel that human affairs, particularly on a large scale, are too often taken over by strange alien forces which insinuate themselves into control in ways too subtle and well organised to be explained by mere human planning and ingenuity. Once in control they can bring about the oppression and destruction of human life, liberty and goodness on an enormous scale, and spoil the best plans of those who cherish openness and truth. They feel, too, that in personal life 'to speak of the dominion of sin and Satan is to speak of what human experiences knows to be true.'[27]

Heim's theory moreover has a healthy objectivity in its description of the work of Christ. It takes seriously the biblical testimony that sin is hatred of God. It preserves the notes of urgency and solemn warning that are there when the New Testament writers appeal for response to the cross. It can say more about the work of Christ than theories whose background is confined to the return home of a prodigal to the Father's house, or to the bringing of a sacrifice to an altar. It has something that other theories lack: but they too have much that this one lacks.

SOLIDARITY AND INTERCESSION

Occasionally in writings about the atonement we come across the suggestion that Christ's intercessory prayer played a large part in his atoning work. For Abelard intercession explains the whole atonement. Christ interceded with God for us because he loved us. How can God refuse to answer such a prayer?[28] Others bring in the thought of intercession differently. Calvin speaks of the intercession of Christ's righteousness by which God reconciles and justifies us.[29] In McLeod Campbell's view Christ accompanied his confession of our sins by an intercession which was his response to the divine yearnings for us, and by which he 'laid hold of God's forgiveness to draw it forth'. Such intercession was 'a fitting form of his bearing over burdens'.[30] In more recent times T. F. Torrance speaks of Christ's human prayer as 'an essential part of his atoning obedience offered to the Father'. Before we conclude our theological guidelines we must follow up these points as far as we can.

Christ's intercession for us arose out of both the one-ness he felt with us, and the oneness he felt with God. Jesus grew up, as is normal, with a sense of solidarity with his family, his local community and his place within it, and with his nation. But he also had a deep, never-failing sense of close relation to God – sometimes called his 'filial consciousness'. This was there very early in his life, as Luke assures us in his story about the boyhood disputation in the temple (Luke 2:45 ff).

A. B. Macaulay suggests that it must have caused him a great deal of perplexity and inward conflict to grow up with such an intimate knowledge of God lying alongside a developing knowledge of the life around him in which he was also deeply involved. He must have been often saddened by the sickness and tragedies that happened in the lives around him. But he must, too, have discovered around him things that hurt uniquely. It was an ordinary sinful environment, and his sense of God must have prompted him to intervention, and to witness to his Father in situations 'where deeds of which he approved or disapproved were done'. What kind of reception did such intervention have? He would gradually discover, suggests Macaulay, the deep hold which the spirit of enmity against his Father's will had on those around him. And the malignity of the opposition he was bound to encounter would give him a foretaste of things to come when he left home finally to begin his active ministry.[31]

Whether such feelings can be legitimately traced to his childhood or not, there undoubtedly came a time when his sympathy with the sorrows and horror of the sins of those with whom he was one would have found expression in agonising intercessory prayer to his Father.

We can find a helpful example of how such prayer can arise from such a burden in the *Journal* of John Woolman the Quaker. A footnote to the *Journal* gives a description of Woolman by John Greenleaf Whittier: 'His singular conscientious scruples, his close self-question-

ings are prompted by a tender concern for universal well being. . . .
He offered no prayers for personal favours. He was, to use his own
words, mixed with his fellow creatures in their misery, and could not
consider himself a distinct or separate being.' Woolman records one of
his last prayers, for 29th Sept. 1772:

> O Lord my God! The amazing horrors of darkness were gathered
> around me, and covered me all over, and I saw no way to go forth.
> I felt the depth and extent of the misery of my fellow creatures
> separated from the divine harmony, and it was heavier than I could
> bear and I was crushed down under it. I lifted up my hand, I
> stretched out my arm, and there was none to help me: I looked
> round about and was amazed.[32]

Such compassion, horror and burden of heart as we see in Woolman
were no doubt reflected in him from Christ himself. But when we look
directly at Christ's intercession we find other important ingredients.
For Jesus (as often with the psalmists) prayer was a cry for justice and
for the vindication of righteousness on the earth (cf. Ps. 68; 94; Luke
18:1 ff). It was also an entry into combat with the powers of evil that
he knew held humanity in bondage. Jesus refused to accept the necessity of the evils of earth. As long as he had any means of removing them
he rebelled against disease, corruption and all social wrong.[33] Prayer
was for him a weapon in the fight for the abolition of the works of evil
and the destruction of the evil one. He refused to let go of what evil
wanted, and refused to accept what evil was doing in this world. With
such defiance he went before God.

His rebellion against evil began in prayer, and through daring such
prayer, he committed himself before God to complete bitter conflict
between himself and the evil one, and hastened the issues that were to
bring such agony to himself. Moreover, his compassion, horror and
rebellion built up a pressure on God – even a combat with God – to
remove such evils more speedily than he had promised. In the cry for
our deliverance, raised by Jesus in his intercession for us, the case for
humanity was brought before God in heaven with a new intensity. God
was prepared to receive pressure from Jesus to act. It is one of the
characteristics of the God of the Bible that he loves the fellowship of
people coming to ask him to do things for them. A reason for the
incarnation was that God might have the case for humanity brought
before him with all the urgency it demanded.

Hooker suggests that the incarnation took place not only that Christ
might offer a sacrifice in human nature from us but that also he might

make intercession for us. 'He which without our nature could not on earth suffer for the sins of the world doth now also, by means thereof . . . make intercession to God for sinners.'[34] There is a strange paradox here. The weaker and more broken the intercessor, the more willing is God to be taken hold of and conquered. God resists the proud, the self-willed, those who have independent resources and their own ground to stand on in their approach to him. But when the pleader is utterly trustful, utterly weak, utterly surrendered and broken under the will of God – as Jesus was – then God is overcome. It can indeed be a rule of all prayer that 'as God prevails over us, we prevail with God.'[35]

In Christ's intercessory prayers for mankind we seem to have all the ingredients that went into his atoning work – a pleading, heart-breaking love for the wayward, sinful individual; the cry for righteousness to be vindicated and for evil to be condemned at all costs; an unrelenting commitment to the final defeat of all evil powers; and impatient conflict with God in the faith that he will bring things to a speedy issue. P. T. Forsyth is right to say that 'the soul of the atonement is prayer.'[36] For Jesus to 'bear the sin of many, and to make intercession for the transgressors' on earth are not two separate actions, but one.

Christ's intercession continues in a new, different way in heaven. The personal human agony of Christ is over; his battle has been won. He has finished the work God gave him to do (John 17:4). We accept the distinction normally made between the nature of Christ's earthly and heavenly intercessions. The latter is not the continuation of what Christ did on the cross, nor the consummation of his sacrifice, nor even a part of it. It could be called the 'prolonged energy of his redeeming work'.[37] It is a pleading and proclamation of his sacrifice. It helps to effect what has been already done. In the words of John Owen, he 'presents himself so that his former oblation might have its perpetual efficacy'.[38]

Notes

CHAPTER 1 (pp. 1–17)

1 Cf. G. von Rad, *Old Testament Theology* (1975), I, p. 263; A. B. Davidson, *The Theology of the Old Testament* (1904), p. 207.
2 Cf. Davidson, op. cit., pp. 315–18; W. Eichrodt, *Theology of the Old Testament* (1961), I, pp. 161–2. Throughout the book of Leviticus it is stressed that the sins provided for in the cult are those committed unwittingly, e.g. 4:1,13,22,27. Provision is also made for more serious sins, e.g. 6:2, where a 'breach of faith against the Lord' is mentioned (in NEB a 'grievous fault'). But in Num. 15:30 it is prescribed that if a person sins 'with a high hand' (NEB 'presumptuously') he is to be cut off from among God's people 'because he has despised the Word of the Lord'. Possibly the affair of Num. 14:40–4 (cf. Deut. 1:43) is an example of such defiance. Cf. also H. H. Rowley, *Worship in Ancient Israel: its Forms and Meanings* (1967), pp. 132–4.
3 Cf. esp. von Rad, op. cit., I, pp. 263–71.
4 The chief word used for what happens to sin through the sacrifices is *kaphar*, cf. Ps. 78:38; 79:9; 85:3. It means primarily to make expiation for sin by purging it, coming from a root meaning to wipe out, to cover, or wash away, though some scholars, e.g. Vriezen, think the original root might be to smooth or to spread, and there are hints at times that it can be used of placating someone, cf. Prov. 16:14, as Jacob appeased Esau in Gen. 32, i.e., of wiping the anger from the face of a person. 'Cover' could also mean, as A. B. Davidson points out, 'the withdrawing of its power to provoke the anger of God' (cf. Isa. 45:22, Mic. 7:19). 'But', he adds, 'God does not cover, and then forgive. The atoning covering is a figure of forgiveness', op. cit., pp. 323, 329.
5 T. C. Vriezen, *An Outline of Old Testament Theology* (1958), p. 281; cf. Eichrodt, op. cit., I, p. 176.
6 Cf. 2 Kgs. 3:27. There are cases in the Old Testament narrative in which some form of expiation is made, and the anger of God is mentioned, e.g. Num. 16:1–40; 25:6–12. An offering suggesting propitiation is suggested in David's conversation with Saul in 1 Sam. 26:19, cf. Gen. 8:21. But it remains the remarkable fact that God never appears as the object of the verb *kaphar*, cf. R. Kittel, *Theological Wordbook of the New Testament*, III, pp. 304f.
7 Von Rad, op. cit., I, p. 260.
8 For the 'sin-offering' see Lev. 4:1–35; 6:24–30; for the 'guilt offering' see Lev. 5:14–6:7; 7:1–10. For any layman the writings of the experts on these sacrificial offerings are contradictory and full of confusion.
9 Cf. Rowley, op. cit., p. 130.
10 Eichrodt, op. cit., I, p. 160.
11 Cf. F. C. N. Hicks, *The Fullness of Sacrifice* (1930), p. 14.

12 A. B. Davidson finds such ideas early in Israel's life (op. cit., p. 355), but questions whether they are found in the Law (p. 354), though he finds that 'deep and mystical ideas gathered round the blood' and 'there were grounds they did not see' which the future might reveal.

13 Rowley, op. cit., pp. 92–3.

14 Vriezen, op. cit., pp. 291–2. Eichrodt, too, insists that the rites are simply a 'free and gracious ordinance of the covenant, requiring trustful obedience', op. cit. I, p. 160. Von Rad regards the secrecy with which God works in sacrifice as deliberate, and affirms that it is 'precisely the most important aspect of the sacrifice' which takes place (designedly) beyond the limit of human explanation. Op. cit., I, p. 260.

15 Cf. p. 00 – though at a later time it seems to have been taught among the Rabbis that the Day of Atonement could deal with sins 'committed with a high hand', cf. Rowley, op. cit., p. 134.

16 Karl Barth, *Church Dogmatics*, II/1, p. 366.

17 Isa. 54:7–8; Ps. 30:5; Hos. 11:9; cf. Barth, op. cit., II, 1 p. 373.

18 Davidson, op. cit., p. 332.

19 A. Weiser, *The Psalms* (1959), p. 270.

20 S. H. Hooke, *Alpha and Omega* (1961), p. 44.

21 Von Rad (op. cit., I, p. 248; II, p. 403) makes this point, and says, 'ultimately the whole ministry of the priesthood was a ministry of vicarious mediation.'

22 Ibid., II, p. 403.

23 W. Eichrodt, *Ezekiel* (1970), p. 33.

24 Von Rad, op. cit., II, pp. 232–3. S. H. Hooke (op. cit., p. 80) points out God, too, shares the agony. He quotes the RV marginal reading of Amos 2:13 adopted by the NEB: 'I groan under the burden of you, as a wagon creaks under a full load.'

25 Von Rad, op. cit., II, pp. 403–4.

26 Cf. Jer. 42:2ff; 27:28; Gen. 20:7; and Eichrodt, op. cit., I, p. 167. That the prophets and other devout persons could plead for their people, and that through their prayers atonement could be made for the nation's transgressions, was a general conviction (Gen. 18:23; Exod. 32:11–14; 1 Sam. 12:22; Amos 7:2,5; Jer. 7:16; 11:14; 14:11; 15:1,11; Ezek. 13:5; 14:14; 22:30).

27 Davidson, op. cit., pp. 337–8.

28 Cf. von Rad's account of this change in prophecy in the 8th century prophets, op. cit., II, p. 185.

29 E. Earle Ellis, *St Paul's use of the Old Testament* (1959), pp. 127–8; cf. *Essays in Old Testament Interpretation*, ed. Claus Westermann (1963), p. 36; G. W. H. Lampe and K. J. Woolacombe, *Essays on Typology*, (1957) p. 39.

30 Von Rad, op. cit., II, p. 330.

31 Hooke, op. cit., p. 90.

32 Von Rad, op. cit., II, pp. 403–4. There is a school of thought which regards these servant songs as containing simply a description of the true Israel.

33 Hooke, op. cit., p. 90.

CHAPTER 2 (pp. 18–31)

1 Cf. John 1: 29. John may be referring to Jesus as the true passover lamb (Exod. 12:5) or to Isa. 53:7. It is more tempting, however, to think of him as referring to Gen. 22:13.

2 Cf. Luke 7:19; Matt. 11:1–6. Since John, clearly, in his own mind and in that of Jesus, had fulfilled the role of Elijah, it could be inferred that Jesus might have about him some of the characteristics of Elijah's successor Elisha. There may be in the cryptic saying of Jesus a hint to John to notice that he was frequently engaged in exactly the same kind of work as Elisha formerly excelled in.

3 Mark 16:21; 10:38. A. M. Hunter points out that out of 20 metaphorical uses of the word 'cup' in the Old Testament, in 17 it is used as a metaphor for divinely appointed suffering (*Words and Works of Jesus* (1963), p. 96). In the traditional use of four cups at the Passover feast authority for the cups of blessing was found in Pss. 16:15; 23:5 and 116:3, it being imagined that the use of the plural in Ps. 116:3 implied two cups! These cups of blessing were contrasted especially with four cups of wrath reserved for the nations. Jer. 25:15; Isa. 51:17; Ps. 11:6; 75:8.

4 Matt. 24:26; NEB, 'the way appointed for him in the Scriptures'.

5 Cf. John 19:23, 28, 36; cf. also Luke 4:21. His cleansing of the temple, e.g., was the fulfilment of Mal. 3:1–2, and other texts. His entry into Jerusalem was staged to conform to Zech. 9:9.

6 This view of an aspect of Christ's human experience will offend those who insist (often with the implication that all who disagree are heretics!) that in every respect Jesus must have shared *exactly* all our own experiences (*except*, of course, that of sinning). Otherwise, it is asserted, he could not have been human. We find that we do not read of such a Christ in the Gospels. We have to insist that Jesus was human as we are, yet with the humanity he is shown to have had in the Gospels.

7 Is it not our experience that what brings him so close to us ourselves as we read the Gospels is the fact that he is one who is so different from us all, and who, yet (thank God!) wants to give us what we lack? On Jesus' own part, he seems to be in agony over us unless we open our lives for him to share with us what he has to give.

8 Cf. his feeling in Mark 5:30 that 'power had gone out of him'.

9 Luke 5:12–17. I owe this insight to a very helpful sermon I heard from my friend the Rev. Norman Logan.

10 It is significant that Jesus' first and clearly distinct word to this man in such urgent physical need was 'Your sins are forgiven' (cf. Luke 12:15).

11 Cf. T. W. Manson, *The Teaching of Jesus* (1931), p. 235: 'Over against the Kingdom of God stands the Kingdom of Satan: and between these two Kingdoms there is war . . . In the life of Jesus . . . the conflict . . . is brought to a decisive issue.' Markus Barth points out that a highly probable version of Eph. 2:15–16 could imply that the battle in which the Messiah was engaged took place decisively within himself too. Cf. the Jerusalem Bible translation: 'He killed the enmity in his own person.' Therefore the peace and blessing which Jesus could impart to others were won and kept over against an inner tension that was felt acutely even as he faced the cross.

12 Yet even in the middle of his trial Jesus reminded his persecutors that they derived the very power they were abusing from God himself. 'You would have no power over me,' he said to Pilate, 'unless it had been given you from above; therefore he who delivered me to you has no greater sin' (John 19:11). It is highly significant for our understanding of Paul's thought later, that the authorities claimed that they had the *law* on their side in killing Jesus: 'We have a law and by that law he ought to die' (John 19:7), i.e. the powers of evil, in the battle against Jesus, entrenched themselves in the law; cf. W. Pannenberg, *Jesus, God and Man*, pp. 253–4.

13 Rev. 19:13ff. It is a striking feature of the book of Revelation that though the stage is set for the final battle (of Armageddon) it does not seem to take place at all. Nothing more seems to be necessary.

CHAPTER 3 (pp. 32–51)

1 We have used this section of the parable *only* as an analogy. The fitness of drawing this analogy deepens when we think of how on Good Friday Jesus was indeed 'a great way off' with the weight of our sins upon him and the Father ran to meet him. Did Jesus here hide himself in this parable as he did in so many others? And do we here have one central point on which we are meant to concentrate? The accompanying parables of the Lost Sheep and the Lost Coin emphasise the turning of God towards us in Christ, and it completes the true picture that these should be accompanied by one that shows also the turning of man towards God *in Christ*. It is true that the parable of the prodigal son has many other lessons to teach – yet it is difficult to avoid this one.

2 Cf. for example Kittell, *TWNT*, III, pp. 316–7.

3 Cf. ibid., I, p. 255.

4 We have already noted how often the New Testament brings out the fact of the *exchange* that takes place between Christ and those for whom he acts as representative and substitute, see pp. 37. This echoes the thought of Isa. 53:5. Paul dwells on this in several places, e.g. 2 Cor. 8:9, and we shall have cause to note it again, see index – 'substitutionary exchange.'

5 H. C. G. Moule, *The Fundamentals* II (Chicago, n.d.), p. 110, quoted Leon Morris *The Cross in the New Testament*, p. 247n.

6 Cf. Morris, ibid., p. 242.

7 C. K. Barrett, commentary on *2 Corinthians* (1973), p. 176.

8 Cf. e.g. Ps. 4:1; 5:8, etc; Isa. 45:8; 61:10–11. cf. James Denney, *The Death of Christ* (1902), pp. 166–9.

9 Cf. Sydney Cave, *The Doctrine of the Work of Christ* (1937), p. 130.

10 Rom. 3:24; it is the NEB which translates 'redemption' as 'liberating act'.

11 John 19:7. Cf. Pannenberg, op. cit., pp. 253–4.

12 Cf. Rom. 7:7; 5:13,20; 4:15. Cf. also V. P. Furnish, *Theology and Ethics in Paul* (1968), pp. 138–41.

13 Though he notes that Paul avoids saying that Jesus was 'accursed by God', James Denney makes the comment: 'Though it is Christian, it is not illogical to avoid such an expression as "accursed of God". For in so making the doom of men his own in death, Christ was doing God's will,' op. cit., p. 162.

14 W. Pannenberg, op. cit., p. 244. We can give Paul's phrase about Christ

being 'born under the law' a great variety of meanings. We have already read it as implying that he was born to bear the curse of the law in the form of its penalty, but it could also imply that he was born with all our temptations to revert to the law as a means of achieving God's grace – in which case we have to look to him as an example and inspiration in living by God's grace. And it could also mean that he was born subject to those who were going to use the law to kill him, and that he had to submit himself to condemnation by a legal process manifestly false – in which case his example and fellowship can give comfort always to what seems to be an ever increasing multitude of people over the world held without trial and condemned without justice.

15 Morris, op. cit., p. 347.
16 Ibid., pp. 349–50.
17 There are possible references in the Old Testament to salvation from sin, cf. Isa. 33:22–4; Ps. 130:8; Ezek. 36:29.
18 1 Cor. 1:22; 5:5; Eph. 1:14; 4:30. Furnish, op. cit., p. 134.
19 Ibid., p. 123.
20 For an excellent discussion of the last point, see M. Barth, *Ephesians* (1974), pp. 115ff.
21 Cf. H. A. A. Kennedy, *St Paul's Conception of the Last Things* (1904).
22 Cf Morris, op. cit., p. 358n.: 'The crucifixion is not regarded simply as a happening that took place and is all over. While there is a once-for-all aspect to it, there is also an aspect which sees it as of permanent validity and continuing effect.'
23 M. Barth, op. cit., I, p. 232.
24 Ibid. loc. cit.

CHAPTER 4 (pp. 52–62)

1 2 Cor. 5:14. NEB, 'The love of Christ leaves us no choice.'
2 Cf. *The Scots Confession* 1560, Art. XIII.
3 Acts 2:38. 'Repent' in its root meaning is 'think again'.
4 Re-telling the story of the cross, especially in preaching, has never failed to make some of its hearers feel, somehow, accountable. This happens today as much as ever it did, cf. the negro spiritual, 'Were you there when they crucified my Lord? Sometimes it causes me to tremble, tremble, tremble.' It is those who feel this accountability who become Christians. Unless it happens to us can we *really* become Christians?
5 Calvin made the text of Matt. 16:24–6 the basis for his description of the life of the Christian.
6 Heb. 2:10. Cf. the drift of the whole chapter.
7 Cf. *Institutes of the Christian Religion*, 2:17:2. Read the whole of this chapter and the next. Cf. Rom. 13:14; Col. 3:5,12; Eph. 3:17; Gal. 2:20.
8 Cf. Andrew Murray: 'The Spirit does not merely come to occupy the place of Jesus, but only wholly to unite the disciples with their Lord more closely . . . than when he was on earth.' *The Full Blessing of Pentecost*, (Lakeland edn., p. 71). Cf. Thomas A. Smail, *Reflected Glory* (1975), pp. 61ff.
9 Gal. 2:20; Rom. 6:5–8; cf. 2 Cor. 5:14. It is difficult to know whether there is any significance in the fact that Paul prefers to speak of our having died, risen, and ascended *with* Christ rather than *in* Christ.

10 D. G. H. Whiteley, *The Theology of St Paul* (1964), pp. 148ff.
11 Manson, op. cit., p. 234.

CHAPTER 5 (pp. 63–74)

1 Constance L. Maynard, *Dora Greenwell* (1926), pp. 212–3.
2 Denney, *Death of Christ*, p. 164.
3 They were aware that what they called the 'fact' of the cross was in itself 'a definite doctrine of what our Lord did', but it was 'not reflective but immediate', attained by 'direct intuition' and calling for reflection. J. Scott Lidgett, *The Spiritual Principle of the Atonement* (1897) p. 121.
4 *Aids to Reflection*, CXVIII, c, 2.
5 Dora Greenwell, *Colloquia Crucis* (1871), p. 87.
6 A. B. Macaulay, *The Death of Christ* (1938), p. 10.
7 Luther's *Works* (*LW*) 26:284.
8 R. S. Franks, *A History of the Doctrine of the Work of Christ* (1918), I, pp. 121, 136.
9 Cf. R. C. Moberly, *Atonement and Personality* (1901), p. 364.
10 See L. W. Grensted, *A Short History of the Doctrine of the Atonement* (1920), pp. 38ff.
11 Ibid., p. 99; Franks, op. cit., I, p. 139.
12 Cf. John M'Intyre, *Anselm and his Critics* (1954), p. 167; Grensted, op. cit., pp. 120–21; Franks, op. cit., I, p. 184.
13 Cf. A. Ritschl, *History and the Doctrine of Justification and Reconciliation* (1872), p. 30.
14 A. C. Welch, *Anselm* (1901), p. 176.
15 Quoted by Franks, op. cit., I, p. 188.
16 Cf. Ritschl, op. cit., pp. 36–8; Franks, op. cit., I, pp. 189–91.
17 Franks, op. cit., p. 92.

CHAPTER 6 (pp. 75–91)

1 A. von Harnack, *History of Dogma* (1896), VI, p. 196. If we tried to do such a thing today, we certainly could produce a vast collection of wonderful insights, from every point of view, but it would be difficult to give any one 'distinct impression' other than of the greatness and majesty of the work of God before us.
2 Franks, op. cit., I, p. 300.
3 ibid., p. 388.
4 J. Kostlin, *The Theology of Luther* (1897), II, p. 389.
5 Quoted Kostlin, II, p. 390.
6 Cf. Kostlin, op. cit., II, p. 405; and Paul Althaus, *The Theology of Martin Luther* (1966), p. 220.
7 Althaus, op. cit., p. 215; *Weimarer Ausgabe*, (*WA*) 29:356, quoted by Althaus, op. cit., p. 217.
8 Cf. Kostlin, op. cit., II, pp. 284, 406.
9 *WA* 31:190–91, quoted by Althaus, op. cit., p. 213.
10 Kostlin, op. cit., II, p. 366.
11 Cf. Althaus, op. cit., p. 202, quoting *WA* 21:264; cf. also *LW* 51:92; 12:365.

12 Cf. Kostlin, op. cit., II, p. 284, 406.
13 *WA* 20:609; cf. Althaus, op. cit., p. 226. The Puritans and Jonathan Edwards followed Luther in seeing the power of the devil linked up with the wrath of God, cf. p. 000.
14 *LW* 12:374. Cf. Kostlin, op. cit., II, pp. 285–6, and Althaus, op. cit., pp. 171–3.
15 Cf. Kostlin, loc. cit.
16 Cf. Althaus, op. cit., p. 171.
17 *LW* 27:4; cf. Kostlin, op. cit., II, p. 396. This one aspect of the theme was taken up by, for example, McLeod Campbell in the nineteenth century, and made central.
18 E.g. in Ps. 40:12; 41:4; 69:5, etc. *LW* 26:279.
19 Cf. Kostlin, op. cit., II, pp. 398–400, *LW* 29:296; also Althaus, op. cit., p. 207.
20 Cf. K. R. Hagenbach, *History of Doctrines* (1847), II, p. 43.
21 Althaus, op. cit., p. 208.
22 *LW* 51:208; cf. Kostlin, op. cit., II, p. 402.
23 Cf. Kostlin, op. cit., II, pp. 368–9; Althaus, op. cit., p. 214.
24 Althaus, op. cit., p. 212.
25 See *LW*, Vol. 35.
26 Kostlin, op. cit., II, pp. 415–6.
27 John Calvin, *Institutes of the Christian Religion*. The edition referred to is that in the Library of Christian Classics (1960).
28 Cf. *LW* 36:177; 51:277.
29 Westminster Confession of Faith, VIII:5.
30 Quoted by H. Lovell Cocks, *The Religious Life of Oliver Cromwell* (1960), p. 73.
31 *The Works of Thomas Goodwin* (1861), V, pp. 188–9.
32 *The Works of Stephen Charnock* (1864), II, p. 323.
33 Goodwin's *Works*, V, p. 189.
34 Ibid., p. 185.
35 Cf. Grensted, op. cit., pp. 282–7.
36 The followers of Jacob Arminius (1560–1609) who stressed the part played by free-will in salvation.
37 *The Works of John Owen* (1852), X, p. 284.
38 The above arguments are given in Owen's work, *The Death of Death in the Death of Christ*, Works X, pp. 139ff. Cf. summary in Franks, op. cit., II, p. 181.
39 Owen's *Works*, X, pp. 269–70. On the matter of limited atonement, see pp. 000 and and my forthcoming work, *The Living Fountain*.
40 Cf. Franks, op. cit., II, p. 181.
41 John McLeod Campbell, *The Nature of Atonement* (1869).
42 Cf. Anselm, *Cur Deus Homo*, I:xx
43 H. Bushnell, *The Vicarious Sacrifice* (1892), p. 68, cf. p. 11.
44 R. W. Dale, *The Atonement* (1897), p. 326.
45 Ibid., p. 372. See the brief account of Dale's views in *Life of R. W. Dale* by his son (1899), p. 713.
46 *Epistle to the Ephesians*, pp. 62–3; *Life*, pp. 708–9.

47 *Christian Doctrine*, quoted by R. S. Paul, *The Atonement and the Sacraments* (1956), p. 205.

CHAPTER 7 (pp. 92–106)

1 Emil Brunner, *The Mediator* (1934), p. 455. Cf. on this matter, Lidgett, op. cit., p. 129 Moberly, op. cit., pp. 324–5 Morris, op. cit., p. 403.
2 e.g. in Phil. 2:5–11 cf. Moberly, op. cit., pp. 147–8.
3 Brunner, op. cit., p. 510.
4 Thomas Goodwin, *Works* v, p. 173.
5 A full discussion of this matter is given in Harry Johnson, *The Humanity of the Saviour* (1962).
6 P. T. Forsyth, *The Cruciality of the Cross* (1909), pp. 139–40.
7 K. Barth, *Church Dogmatics* IV/1, p. 127.
8 Jean Bosc, *The Kingly Office of the Lord Jesus Christ* (1959), p. 13.
9 Ibid. p. 14. Cf. K. Barth, *Church Dogmatics* III/3, p. 275; IV/1, pp. 135–6.
10 T. F. Torrance, *Theology in Reconstruction* (1965), p. 157; *The School of Faith* (1959), p. lxxxiv.
11 A. Wikenhauser, *Pauline Mysticism* (1960), p. 25.
12 *Institutes*, 2:17:1. Cf. Augustine, *On the Gift of Perseverance*, XXIV, 67.
13 H. S. Scott Holland, *Creed and Character* (1892), quoted by Donald MacKinnon, *Borderlands of Theology* (1968), pp. 107–8.
14 Moberly, op. cit., pp. 103, 107. Moberly gives the following lists of texts: John 5:17, 19, 20, 30; 6:57; 8:19, 28, 29, 38; 9:4; 10:37, 38; 14:10. Cf. James Denney, *The Christian Doctrine of Reconciliation* (1917), p. 233.
15 K. Barth, *Church Dogmatics*, IV2, p. 92., cf. p. 96.
16 Cf. M. J. Scheeben, *The Mysteries of Christianity* (1946), p. 327, 'If Christs humanity had sinned, the sinful act would have been ascribed to the divine person to whom the humanity belongs.'
17 Moberly, op. cit., p. 107.
18 Hebrews 5:8. Calvin, *Institutes*, 2:16:5, Moberly, op. cit. p. 106.
19 Forsyth, op. cit., p. 203–4. Cf. Hans W. Frei, *The Identity of Jesus Christ* (1975), p. 107. Frei stresses that Jesus' obedience was a counterpart to his being sent and that we find the centre of Jesus' person not within himself but in his story.
20 Brunner, op. cit., p. 501.
21 Cf. Brunner, op. cit., p. 496; R. S. Paul, op. cit., p. 167; Lidgett, op. cit., p. 147.
22 John 10:17f. Cf. Brunner, op. cit., p. 511.
23 Pannenberg, op. cit., pp. 245, 277.
24 Brunner, op. cit., p. 511.
25 Frei, op. cit., pp. 103–4.
26 Campbell, op. cit., p. xix.
27 Goodwin's *Works*, v, p. 193. Goodwin here makes a fine and difficult distinction between the sickness that Christ bore 'personally', i.e., by reason of the divine-human person that he was, and those he bore 'out of such sympathy'.
28 *The Works of Jonathan Edwards* (1834) II, *On Satisfaction for Sin*, p. 575.
29 Goodwin's *Works*, v, 198, 284.
30 Ibid., v, 190, 194. John Owen (*Works*, X, p. 179) speaks of 'His subjection

to the curse of the law, in the antecedent suffering of life as well as by submitting to death, the death of the Cross.'

31 Edwards, *Works*, II, 575. The Puritans, too, linked the devil closely to the wrath of God.

32 Ibid., loc. cit. Edwards states that 'Christ was given by the Spirit of God a "great and dreadful" sense of the odiousness of sin' which increased his revulsion and aversion to what he was bearing on the cross – this in addition to 'the bitter fruit and consequences of sin'.

33 Quoted by Franks, op. cit., II, p. 389; for a helpful account of the thought of Maurice on this matter, see Moberly, op. cit., pp. 384–5.

34 Pannenberg, op. cit., p. 279.

35 Bushnell, op. cit., p. 34.

36 Heiko Oberman, *The Harvest of Mediaeval Theology* (1967), p. 267.

37 J. M. Wilson, Hulsean Lectures 1887–88, quoted by R. S. Paul, op. cit., p. 223. See Paul's excellent discussion of this matter, loc. cit.

38 G. S. Hendry, *The Gospel of the Incarnation* (1958), pp. 139f., 143. Cf. Morris, op. cit., p. 376.

39 Moberly, op. cit., p. 332.

40 Max Warren, *Interpreting the Cross* (1966), p. 81.

41 A. M. Ramsey, *The Gospel and the Catholic Church* (1956), pp. 20–21. Cf. Brunner, op. cit., p. 441: 'To be born into this life . . . is still in itself something beautiful . . . But the Cross is in every respect hideous.'

42 James Denney, *The Atonement and the Modern Mind*, (1910), p. 109. Cf. R. S. Paul, op. cit., p. 209, and Moltmann, *The Crucified God* (1974), pp. 204–5.

43 Owen, *Works*, X, 172.

44 Pannenberg, op. cit., pp. 269–73; cf. A. B. Macaulay, *The Death of Jesus* (1938), pp. 127ff.

45 Macaulay, op. cit., p. 136; cf. Moberly, op. cit., 128, 130.

46 P. T. Forsyth, *The Justification of God* (1948 edn.), p. 26.

47 Goodwin, *Works*, V, p. 194.

48 K. Barth, *Church Dogmatics* II/2, p. 749.

49 Cf. R. S. Wallace, *Many Things in Parables* (1955), pp. 3–40.

50 A. E. Taylor, *The Faith of a Moralist* (1930), II, p. 129.

51 J. Calvin, *Commentary on Hebrews*, 6:19.

52 Jacques Bossuet, *Jesus*, quoted by A. B. Macaulay, op. cit., p. 132.

53 H. R. Mackintosh, *The Doctrine of The Person of Jesus Christ* (1971), p. 403.

54 Karl Heim, *The Church of Christ and the Problems of Today* (1936), pp. 95–6.

55 Von Rad, op. cit., I, p. 260, cf. p. 253.

56 Heim, op. cit., p. 96.

57 P. T. Forsyth, *The Holy Father and the Living Christ* (1897), p. 65; cf. Brunner, op. cit., pp. 504–5: 'This event does not belong to the historical plane. It is super-history. It lies in the dimension which no historian knows insofar as he is merely a historian.' Cf. also Moberly, op. cit., p. 389.

58 Forsyth, *The Cruciality of the Cross*, p. 99; cf. A. C. Quick, *Doctrines of the Creed*, (1938), p. 78.

59 Pannenberg, op. cit., p. 48.

60 *LW* 26:282. Cf. Kostlin, op. cit., II, p. 366.

61 Gustav Aulén, *Christus Victor* (1950), p. 50.

62 This is not *always* the case with Luther; cf. *LW* 51:62, 'God has chosen *a man*, the Lord Jesus Christ, to crush death' . . . etc.

63 *Institutes*, 2:17: 1 & 2. Pannenberg asserts that after Luther, Calvin returned to Anselm's view with the proviso that not the man, but the divine-human person accomplishes the salvation, op. cit., p. 280.

64 Aulén, op. cit., p. 137.

CHAPTER 8 (pp. 107–111)

1 F. D. Maurice, *Theological Essays* (1853), pp. 113–4.

2 Quoted by Max Warren, op. cit., pp. 22–3.

3 Barth, *Church Dogmatics* II/1, p. 360.

4 Maurice, op. cit., p. 109.

5 Moberley, op. cit., p. 90, 130.

6 Forsyth, *Work of Christ*, pp. 149–50; cf. Paul, op. cit., p. 237.

7 Forsyth, *Cruciality of the Cross*, p. 78.

8 Dietrich Bonhoeffer, *The Cost of Discipleship* (1959), p. 214; cf. Scheeben, op. cit., pp. 354, 366; Brunner, op. cit., p. 503.

9 Quick, op. cit. p. 84.

10 Moltmann, op. cit. pp. 261ff.

11 Campbell, op. cit., p. 141.

12 Althaus, op. cit., p. 87.

13 Aulén, op. cit., p. 171.

14 Barth, *Church Dogmatics*, II/1, p. 274.

15 Aulén, op. cit., p. 171.

16 Heim, op. cit., p. 95.

17 Cf. Paul, op. cit., pp. 158, 173.

18 Bushnell, op. cit., pp. 35–6.

19 C. A. Dinsmore, *The Atonement in Literature and Life* (1906), p. 232f.; cf. Morris op. cit., p. 278.

20 D. M. Baillie, *God was in Christ* (1948), p. 200.

21 Ibid., p. 201.

22 Ibid., pp. 195–6.

23 Quoted by W. R. Mueller, *John Donne; Preacher* (1962), pp. 111ff.

CHAPTER 9 (pp. 112–125)

1 Heim, *Jesus the World's Perfector* (1959) p. 87.

2 Lidgett, op. cit., pp. 394–5.

3 J. G. Riddell, *Why did Jesus die?* (1938), pp. 111–3.

4 Isaiah 45.21, see pp. 39, 129 and A. E. Taylor, op. cit., I pp. 190–1.

5 Campbell, op. cit., p. 69.

6 Quoted Grensted, op. cit., p. 324.

7 Shedd is quoted as an example of this by Grensted, op. cit., p. 311, 'The claim of law is absolute and indispensable. The eternal judge may or may not exercise mercy; but He must exercise justice.' *Dogmatic Theology* II, p. 436.

8 Owen, *Works* X, p. 205. Though of course for Owen, after God *decreed* to save 'by way of vindictive justice', it was impossible for him to do otherwise.

9 Brunner op. cit., pp. 444–5.
10 Ibid., p. 481.
11 For the difficulties in regarding punishment as other than retributive, see Morris, op. cit., p. 385; A. E. Taylor, op. cit., I, 182–3; L. Hodgson, *The Doctrine of the Atonement* (1951), p. 54.
12 Forsyth, *Work of Christ*, pp. 169–70.
13 Anselm, *Cur Deus Homo*, 1.21; cf. Grensted, op. cit., p. 311; cf. also Owen, *Works* X, pp. 269–70.
14 Brunner, op. cit., p. 481.
15 A. B. Bruce, *The Training of the Twelve* (1901), p. 29f.
16 Scott Lidgett, op. cit., p. 393; cf. Moberly, op. cit., pp. 99–100; Forsyth, *Cruciality of the Cross*, p. 138.
17 Cf. Macaulay, op. cit., 157–8; Morris, op. cit., 408–9.
18 Heinrich Vogel, *The Iron Ration of a Christian*, quoted by Morris, op. cit., p. 414.
19 Cf. Morris, op. cit., p. 410; Pannenberg, op. cit., p. 264.
20 James Orr, *Progress of Dogma* (1908), p. 341.
21 Athanasius, *On the Incarnation*, §7.
22 Greenwell, op. cit., p. 131.
23 P. T. Forsyth, *The Justification of God*, p. 25; cf. Paul, op. cit., p. 233.
24 Cf. Althaus op. cit., p. 219.
25 Cf. Morris, op. cit., p. 381; Aulén, op. cit., p. 70.
26 Forsyth, *Cruciality of the Cross*, p. 117.
27 Moberly, op. cit., p. 339.
28 Cf. A. Ritschl, op. cit., p. 40.
29 *Institutes*, 3.14.9; 3.11.23.
30 Campbell, *Nature of the Atonement*, pp. 147–9, 231–2.
31 Cf. Macaulay, op. cit., pp. 91–2.
32 *The Journal of John Woolman* (Books for the Heart edn.), pp. 305–6.
33 Cf. e.g. D. S. Cairns, *The Faith that Rebels* (1933).
34 *Treatise on the Laws of Ecclesiastical Polity*, V, LI.
35 Cf. Andrew Murray, *The Ministry of Intercession* (Lakeland edn.), p. 41; also Dora Greenwell, *Prayer*, and P. T. Forsyth, *The Soul of Prayer* (Little Books on Religion), pp. 135–7.
36 Forsyth, *The Holy Father and the Living Christ*, p. 141.
37 Forsyth, ibid., pp. 142–3.
38 Owen, *Works*, X, pp. 181–4.

Select Bibliography

1. Books on Biblical Theology
Studies of the old Testament by e.g. A. B. Davidson, W. Eichrodt, E. Jacob, G. von Rad, H. H. Rowley and C. Vriezen contain material; so also do the theologies of the New Testament, e.g. by J. Jeremias, W. G. Kümmel, R. Bultmann, G. E. Ladd and A. Richardson. Then studies of Paul's theology by H. Ridderbos and D. H. Whiteley are important also.

2. Specific Biblical Studies relating to Atonement
F. F. Bruce, *What the Bible says about the Work of Christ* (1979)
J. Denney, *The Death of Christ* (ed. R. V. G. Tasker, 1951)
I. H. Marshall, *The Work of Christ* (1968)
L. Morris, *The Apostolic Preaching of the Cross* (1955)
L. Morris, *The Cross in the New Testament* (1967)
W. Wheeler Robinson, *The Cross in the Old Testament* (1955)
G. Smeaton, *Atonement as taught by Christ and his Apostles* (1871, reprinted 1951)
V. Taylor, *Jesus and his Sacrifice* (1939)
R. de Vaux, *Studies in Old Testament Sacrifice* (1964)

3. Books dealing with the Atonement as a doctrine
Anselm, *Cur Deus Homo* (available in several translations)
Athanasius, *De Incarnatione* (available in several translations)
G. Aulén, *Christus Victor* (1931)
D. M. Baillie, *God was in Christ* (1956)
K. Barth, *Church Dogmatics*, IV, 1–3 (1957–62)
E. Brunner, *The Mediator* (1934)
J. Calvin, *Institutes of the Christian Religion* (Library of Christian Classics, 1960)
J. McLeod Campbell, *The Nature of Atonement* (4th edn. 1959)
R. W. Dale, *The Atonement* (1876)
C. A. Dinsmore, *Atonement in Literature and Life* (1906)
P. T. Forsyth, *The Cruciality of the Cross* (1909)
P. T. Forsyth, *The Work of Christ* (1910)
D. Greenwell, *Colloquia Crucis* (1871)
L. Hodgson, *The Doctrine of Atonement* (1951)
K. Heim, *Jesus the World's Perfector* (1959)
K. Heim, *Jesus the Lord* (1959)
W. Kasper, *Jesus the Christ* (1978)
J. Scott Lidgett, *The Spiritual Principle of the Atonement* (1897)
R. C. Moberly, *The Atonement and Personality* (1901)
J. K. Mozley, *The Atonement* (1937)
J. Owen, *The Death of Death in the Death of Christ* (1647; edited by J. I. Packer, 1959)

Select Bibliography

J. I. Packer, *What did the Cross Achieve?* (1977)

4. Histories of the Doctrine
There is important material in the *The Christian Tradition* (5 vols) by J. Pelikan which is in the process of being published. All general histories of doctrine – e.g. by L. Berkhof, K. Hagenbach, A. von Harnack – have appropriate material.

See especially:

R. S. Franks, *History of the Doctrine of the Work of Christ* (1918)
L. W. Grensted, *A Short History of the Doctrine of the Atonement* (1920)
H. E. W. Turner, *The Patristic Doctrine of Redemption* (1952)

Index of central themes

Atonement

Fact and theory, 64. Cross, a mystery 64f, 100; yet intelligible, 65f; danger of our simplification 71f, 84. Theories inadequate 65, 77, 93, 122. For Mani theories see under 'Penal substitution', 'Sacrifice', 'Victory of Christ', 'love of God'. For theory of vicarious confession or penitence see 35, 85f, 88–9, 108. For 'Limited atonement' see 46f, 85f.

Cost of Atonement

36, 39, 45, 62, 72, 82, 110, 118

Christ in the Atonement

His humanity, fallen 94; inclusive 76–91, 107, 109. Our representative 17, 27, 35, 59, 69, 76, 83, 109, 116–7. Person and Work 66, 102ft. Value of orthodox Christology 106. Participation of Christ's natures in atonement 72, 81ff, 105f, 135.

See also obedience, suffering, vocation, victory of Christ.

Effect of Cross

Faith, 68. Union with Christ, 35f, 37, 60, 63, 68, 76, 78, 91. Justification, 32f, 37ff. Imputation of righteousness, 83, 91, 116. Sanctification 32, 52, 57ff. Regeneration 32f, 47. Spirit of sonship 36, 43, 88f. In history 38f, 49f. Gratitude 53f. Moral influence 73. Salvation, present and future 47ff.

Evil

Sin; nature of 1, 2, 34, 120; consequences of, 7, 37, 40f, 50f, 69, 90, 113–4, 173. Solidarity in sin 117. Guilt 2ff, 6f, 16, 27, 69, 79. The 'Flesh' and sin 41.

Evil powers personal 69f, 118. Satanic Kingdom 28f, 119, 128. Satanic hatred in 'world' 52, 120. Strength of evil revealed in Cross 118, 120. Evil expressed as defeated 118, 121. Redemption from devil 30f, 41, 44f, 69ff. Salvation from death and corruption 41, 61f, 67ff, 81, 122. Evil powers deceived at Cross 43f, 69ff, 77, 121.

Fatherhood of God

22ff, 34f, 37, 81, 87ff, 90.

Freedom of God

In atonement 75, 113; see 'necessity of atonement'.

Fulfilment of Old Testament in Cross

Christ foreshadowed in O.T. 4, 13ff, 16, 57f, 103, 107f. Fulfilment 19, 24, 27, 57ff, 128. Typology 13. New Exodus 7, 13, 16, 19f, 47. New Creation 14, 32ff. Messianic age 13, 19f, 21, 47. Remnant 16f, 20, 27, 61.

God

See: 'Fatherhood', 'Freedom', 'Love', 'Righteousness', 'Suffering', 'Wrath' of God.

Index of central themes

Incarnation and Atonement

43, 56, 67f, 71, 81, 93ff, 97, 103. Incarnation as atonement 94f, 100f. Incarnational union 67f, 81. See 'obedience', 'suffering' of Christ.

Intercession of Christ

In atonement 23, 26, 29, 46, 57, 63, 82, 87, 89, 111, 122f, 125. Heavenly intercession 125. Old Testament intercession 8ff, 14f. See 'suffering' and intercession.

Justification

Atonement as act of 37ff. See 'Law', 'Effect' of atonement.

Law

Law and God 42, 83, 90, 112. Law and love 37, 112f. Christ under law 43, 129f. Powers of evil entrenched in law 30, 42, 129. Law and sin 42. Redemption from curse of law 43. Law and conscience 79, 90.

Love of God

45ff, 64, 70f, 75f, 82. Dual constraint of love and wrath in God 36, 50f, 79, 89, 91, 108, 110. Cross as a demonstration of love 32, 45f, 53, 68, 70f, 73f, 110.

Necessity of the Cross

72, 75, 90, 113

Obedience of Christ

Jesus' whole life atoning 76, 82f. Sinlessness 95. Commitment 54. Obedience 56, 67-8, 72, 76, 81, 83, 95f, 99f. Passive and active obedience 56, 83, 96f. Obedience as miracle of grace 95.

Penal Substitution

The theory in history 83ff, 90. Arguments for and against 87, 89, 112ff, 114, 121. Vicarious punishment 4f, 26, 73, 82f. Christ as bearing penalty 2, 40, 43, 72, 75, 85. Element of retribution 90, 114. Question of equivalent penalty 73, 76, 84f. See substitutionary exchange, sufferings of Christ (cup, baptism).

Preaching of the Cross

53, 130.

Ransom

Place of ransom in O.T. 6-7. Death of Jesus as ransom 26-7. Ransom theory of atonement 69f, 71, 77f. See 'Evil'.

Reconciliation

Element of Reconciliation in atonement 32ff. Heart of atonement 107ff. Forgiveness 5, 7, 32. See 'love of God', 'Sacrifice of Christ'.

Redemption

Atonement as Redemption 27, 32, 40ff, 69ff, 118ff. See 'Evil'.

Index of central themes

Vocation of Christ in Cross

21ff. A way found in Scripture 23f. Fulfils O.T. as Messiah 14, 21, 96; mediator of covenant 27; prophet 10, 83, 85, 27; Priest 8f, 82f, 27; King 12, 83; Son of Man 27, cf 17, 59; Servant and sin-bearer 15, 26, 53f, 101; second Adam 56, 59, 67, 109. Jesus' desire to save 26. Sense of vocation 21–2, 94, 96, 105. Self-consecration and -offering 24f, 57ff. Sense of constraint 52. 'Cup' 23, 26, 27f, 61f. 'Baptism' 22ff, 28, 61.

Wrath (anger) of God

Expressed in atonement 5, 7, 38, 40, 50, 79, 81, 98, 101, 108, 120, 126. (See also 'love of God'). Wrath of God and the devil 79, 98, 132, 135. Deliverance from wrath 58ff.

References to Holy Scripture

Index of names